"LESSONS" OF THE PAST

"LESSONS" OF THE PAST
The Use and Misuse of History in American Foreign Policy

ERNEST R. MAY

New York
OXFORD UNIVERSITY PRESS
1973

For John, Susan, and Donna

There is more to understand. Hold
fast to that as the way to freedom.

T. S. ELIOT

Preface

This book has three theses.

The first is that framers of foreign policy are often influenced by beliefs about what history teaches or portends. Sometimes, they perceive problems in terms of analogies from the past. Sometimes, they envision the future either as foreshadowed by historical parallels or as following a straight line from what has recently gone before.

The first four chapters illustrate how such ways of thinking influenced Americans in World War II, the opening phase of the Cold War, the Korean intervention of 1950, and the entanglement in Vietnam.

Some examples further back in time could be added. In the early months of World War I, for instance, President Woodrow Wilson found himself involved in disputes with the British about American rights on the seas. The diary of his close friend, Colonel House, records the President as saying, "Madison and I are the only two Princeton men that have become President. The circumstances of the War of 1812 and now run parallel. I sincerely hope they will not go further." Having this perception, the President acted cautiously.[1]

Examples from other countries could also be cited. In the first two years of World War II, Hitler repeatedly overruled admirals who proposed expanding the submarine offensive. He did so in part out of belief that avoiding incidents like those that had brought the United States into World War I would keep the United States out of World War II.[2] In 1956, the British government confronted Egypt's seizure of the Suez Canal. Anthony Eden, who was then Prime Minister, records that he and his cabinet saw the event as analogous to crises of the 1930's. He writes,

> Success in a number of adventures involving the breaking of agreements in Abyssinia, in the Rhineland, in Austria, in Czechoslovakia, in Albania had persuaded Hitler and Mussolini that the democracies had not the will to resist, that they could now march with the certitude of success from signpost to signpost along the road which led to world dominion. . . . As my colleagues and I surveyed the scene in these autumn months of 1956, we were determined that the like should not come again.[3]

This perception of the situation led Eden and his cabinet to their futile and humiliating effort to retake Suez by force.

Similar evidence from earlier centuries would not necessarily be pertinent. When statesmen of the eighteenth century cited the past, they assumed that human nature was constant and that universal Newtonian laws governed it. Influenced by concepts of evolution, cultural relativism, and the like, men have since become uneasy about citing Greeks, Roman, Saxons, or even contemporary foreigners as examples of how they themselves might behave. Also, education has changed, and ruling elites have become more heterogeneous, with the result that people in government are more hesitant about alluding to events or experience outside of living memory. Evidence of how Jefferson, Lincoln, Palmerston, or Bismarck employed history would not necessarily indicate how statesmen do so today.

Since this book is addressed to contemporaries, especially in

the United States, I have concentrated on the most recent episodes in American history for which there is adequate published
documentation. I hope thus to counter the possible protest,
"This may have been true of them, but it cannot be true of *us*."
For, though I can only prove that history helped to shape the
thinking of some men at some recent points in time, I believe
that it does so regularly and will continue to do so.

The second thesis of this book is that policy-makers ordinarily use history badly. When resorting to an analogy, they
tend to seize upon the first that comes to mind. They do not
search more widely. Nor do they pause to analyze the case,
test its fitness, or even ask in what ways it might be misleading.
Seeing a trend running toward the present, they tend to assume that it will continue into the future, not stopping to consider what produced it or why a linear projection might prove
to be mistaken.

These habits can have important consequences, for they can
affect the way statesmen understand their situations and problems. There is a simple psychological experiment in which one
looks through a peephole at a room with uneven sides. Accus-
tomed to even-sided rooms, most people will not see it as it is.
Instead, they perceive it as square or rectangular and in doing
so misjudge the location and size of objects within it. Even
when told the truth, moreover, most people find it hard to see
the room in its true proportions. A large number of more com-
plicated experiments show the frequency of such "cognitive
dissonance"—that is, instances in which the mind is presented
with information it overlooks, rejects, or actually changes to suit
expectations.[4] Something of the sort probably occurs among
statesmen. Once persuaded that the War of 1812 or World
War I or "totalitarian aggression" is repeating itself, they may
see only facts conforming to such an image.

This book portrays some American policy-makers whose
thinking was thus narrowed and confined. I believe that this is
often the case and that it will continue to be so until people

who govern recognize and cope with their dependence on history.

The third thesis, corollary to the second, is that policy-makers can, if they will, use history more discriminatingly. They can seek alternative analogies and parallels and in doing so reflect on whether a moral seen in one case is a principle exemplified in many. Instead of merely projecting a trend, they can dissect the forces that produced it and ask whether or not those forces will persist with the same vectors.

Some statesmen have, of course, been more imaginative than others. Interested in how personal courage manifested itself in American politicians, for instance, John F. Kennedy analyzed eight examples. He did so in a book good enough to win a Pulitzer prize.[5] Later, when President and deep in the Cuban missile crisis, he thought not only of Pearl Harbor but also of past European crises. According to his brother, Robert Kennedy, he talked one evening about 1914 and "the miscalculations of the Germans, the Russians, the Austrians, the French, and the British. They somehow seemed to tumble into war, he said, through stupidity, individual idiosyncracies, misunderstandings, and personal complexes of inferiority and grandeur." Further, Robert Kennedy recalled, "We talked about the miscalculation of the Germans in 1939 and the still unfulfilled commitments and guarantees that the British had given to Poland." [6] Although Kennedy was not equally imaginative when thinking about Vietnam, he serves as an example of a statesman who could escape the confines of a single analogy or parallel, even when under intense pressure. Perhaps Richard Nixon, when taking the initiative to relax tensions with China, provided an instance of a statesman liberating himself from belief that a past trend in domestic opinion would necessarily continue into the future.

Not without misgivings, I present in this book two illustrations of how the past might be used more critically and systematically in deliberations on foreign policy. One chapter suggests how examination of past instances of the political use of bombing might have contributed to analysis of whether or not to bomb North Vietnam in 1965. Another chapter draws on the last fifty years of American experience to identify questions involved in forecasting America's posture a decade hence. Because each event and period has so many unique characteristics, such exercises are bound to be exceptionable. The chief claim to be made for them is that, if well done, they might help people who must make choices or must estimate the future to free themselves from the analogies, parallels, or trend-readings which they might otherwise unthinkingly apply.

Even such a limited objective calls for work by analysts sensitive to the variety and complexity of the past, the tentativeness of most historical reconstructions, and the many hazards associated with claiming that one occurrence is "like" another. Such analysts need not be professional historians. It would be enough if some members of policy-makers' staffs had a background in history and its uses comparable to that which many now possess in economics and the manipulation of economic data. Indeed, professional historians might be less well engaged actually participating in government than devising more effective ways of teaching actual or prospective public servants how to think about historical comparisons and projections.

One function strictly for professional historians, however, is the patient assembly and analysis of historical data. If historians are to perform this function well, they must somehow become better able to study those events most likely to influence people in public life—that is, events of the relatively recent past. Even though many of these events may seem as much experience as history, they are susceptible to being better understood if carefully reconstructed—above all if reconstructed by historians of varying approaches who examine the same evidence and dispute about its meaning. In their own interest, statesmen ought not only to make possible but to invite the freest possible documentary and interview research, coming as close as practicable to the present.

Potentially, history is an enormously rich resource for people who govern. If the instances portrayed in this book are at all indicative, such people usually draw upon this resource haphazardly or thoughtlessly. By and large, those of us professionally occupied in teaching and writing history have put out little effort to help them. I hope this book makes some contribution toward advancing cooperation between those who use the past and those who study it.

Cambridge, Mass.   E. R. M.

Contents

ONE

How the Past Has Been Used

I

World War II:
Preparing for the Last Peace

On Christmas eve 1943 tens of millions of Americans listened
on radios to a fireside chat by President Franklin D. Roosevelt. The new armed forces network beamed the broadcast
to the nearly four million American soldiers who had shipped
out since Pearl Harbor for Europe and the Pacific.

Roosevelt had recently returned from a twelve thousand-mile
flight to the Middle East. At Cairo, he and British Prime Minister Winston Churchill had met Generalissimo Chiang Kai-
shek of China. At Teheran, they had conferred with Marshal
Joseph Stalin of the Soviet Union. Reporting on these meetings, Roosevelt said, "We devoted ourselves not only to military matters, we devoted ourselves to consideration of the
future—to plans for the kind of world which alone can justify
all the sacrifices of this war."

Concerning the Far East, the President declared, "Essential
to all peace and security is the elimination of the Empire of
Japan as a potential force of aggression. Never again must our
soldiers and sailors and marines . . . be compelled to fight
from island to island as they are fighting . . . today."

Turning to Europe, Roosevelt described himself, Churchill,

and Stalin as "united in determination that Germany must be
stripped of her military might and be given no opportunity
within the foreseeable future to regain that might." The United
States and the Soviet Union, he predicted, "are going to get
along very well . . . very well indeed." And, while the war-
time allies stuck together, he observed, "there will be no
possibility of an aggressor Nation arising to start another
world war." Summing up, Roosevelt cautioned his audience:

> For too many years we lived on pious hopes that ag-
> gressor and warlike Nations would learn and understand
> and carry out the doctrine of purely voluntary peace.
>   The well-intentioned but ill-fated experiments of former
> years did not work. It is my hope that we will not try
> them again. No—that is putting it too weakly—it is my
> intention to do all that I humanly can as President and
> Commander in Chief to see to it that these tragic mistakes
> shall not be made again.[1]

All Roosevelt's fireside chats were conversational. None,
however, was composed carelessly. In this case as in others,
speechwriters prepared an original version. Roosevelt's closest
personal adviser and negotiator with the British and Russians,
Harry Hopkins, worked it over. Other White House assistants did likewise, attuning nuances to this or that constituency.
Roosevelt meanwhile discussed the substance of what he
planned to say with Secretary of War Henry L. Stimson and
with his old and close friend Secretary of the Treasury Henry
Morgenthau, Jr. This fireside chat went through eight drafts
before the President was finally satisfied.[2] It was not therefore
just Roosevelt's personal utterance; it was a state paper em-
bodying what "the government" was prepared then to say
about the post-war world.

The fireside chat astonished no one. Reporters had trouble
composing front-page stories about it. Anti-administration editors criticized it as commonplace.[3] Yet in retrospect one can-

not read it without amazement. For it completely miscon-strued what was to come.

Not only did Roosevelt make a completely wrong forecast about relations between the United States and the U.S.S.R., but he said, in effect, that Japan and Germany would seem menacing throughout the post-war era. When referring to the "well-intentioned but ill-fated experiments of former years," he seemed to say that the great danger of the future lay in America's once again disarming, promoting pacts such as that which had "outlawed" war, or isolating itself from the affairs of other continents.

In fact, of course, the United States and the Soviet Union were to get along very badly. Japan and Germany were not to revive for a generation. During that same generation the United States was to remain heavily armed, to sign few agree-ments that depended solely on the word of another govern-ment, and to involve itself deeply in the affairs of many other continents.

Why was it that neither the administration nor its critics exhibited insight into the actual future?

One might assume that Americans at the time had no in-timations of what might come. This is not the case. Relations with the Soviet Union had never been cordial. The Soviet government had repeatedly said that it intended to retain Polish territory seized in 1939. Since mid-1943 it had been organizing a communist regime to take control of Poland after the war. At the time of Roosevelt's fireside chat, political commentators were pointing out that the powerful Polish-American bloc in the Northeastern states would probably insist on opposition to Soviet ambitions in Poland.[4] It was at least a foreseeable possibility that this and other issues would soon make the United States and the Soviet Union antagonists rather than partners.

Planning for the war, both private and public, envisioned

complete subjugation of Japan and Germany. Roosevelt had called for their "unconditional surrender." Military officers were hard at work preparing an invasion of Europe which was to end in complete occupation of Germany. Operations in the Pacific looked to landing American troops in Japan. American and British airmen predicted that bombing would meanwhile destroy the economies of both powers. If anything, they exaggerated the probable devastation. It should have been apparent that if Allied plans were carried out neither Japan nor Germany would be a force in international politics for a long time to come.

And polls indicated that both the public and Congress emphatically shared the opinion which Roosevelt expressed in his fireside chat. When asked in April 1943 whether there should be an international police force to preserve peace after the war, 74 per cent said yes and only 14 per cent, no. In September, 87 per cent declared that the United States should maintain larger peace-time armed forces. Not long before, 64 per cent had said the post-war navy should be as large as the navy during the war. And not long afterward, an identical percentage in a representative sample were to declare themselves "internationalists," while only 13 per cent were to identify themselves as "isolationists." [5] It should have seemed more likely than not that these attitudes would persist into the post-war era.

Of course, one might assume that the President and his advisers sensed alternative possibilities but refrained from talking about them because their sole interest was to stir public zeal for the war in hand. We now know a good deal, however, about what was being said in private, and nothing in the record indicates that Roosevelt or his intimates doubted the image of the future delineated in the 1943 fireside chat. To be sure, as the war drew to a close, some officials and commentators openly questioned the probability of good relations with the U.S.S.R. In preparing for the Yalta and San Francisco conferences of 1945, however, the government as a whole continued to assume that the major tasks of the future were to restrain Germany and Japan and, to this end, to ensure that the United States did not retreat into weakness and isolation.

As an explanation of why these erroneous assumptions were so strong and so persistent, I see no alternative to the hypothesis that Americans of this period were captives of an unanalyzed faith that the future would be like the recent past. They visualized World War II as parallel to World War I. They expected its aftermath to be in most respects the same. And they defined statesmanship as doing those things which might have been done to prevent World War II from occurring.

This state of mind was apparent not only in rhetoric but in almost all American preparations for the post-war period—the "unconditional surrender" formula, planning for occupation regimes, the creation of international organizations such as the International Monetary Fund, the World Bank, and the United Nations, and diplomatic negotiations with the Soviet Union.

Americans recalled that in World War I Woodrow Wilson had tried to define precise war aims. The famous Fourteen Points address had been an example. When the Germans accepted his terms, Wilson agreed to an armistice. In retrospect this action was judged to have been ill-advised. Trying to do the exact reverse of what Wilson did, Roosevelt epitomized the Allied objective as simply "unconditional surrender." Although he pretended at the time that the phrase had popped into his mind and out of his mouth during a press conference, he fibbed. In fact, the statement had been weighed before-hand and even cleared with the British cabinet. As White House speechwriter Robert E. Sherwood was to comment, "What Roosevelt was saying was that there would be no negotiated peace, no compromise with Nazism and Fascism, no 'escape clauses' provided by another Fourteen Points which could lead to another Hitler. (The ghost of Woodrow Wilson was again at his shoulder.)" [6]

Although Roosevelt accepted conditional surrender by Italy

in 1943, he and his advisers never considered compromise with Germany. They believed the Germans had not suffered the full consequences of losing World War I. They therefore judged it important that Germany now experienced complete conquest. "It is of the utmost importance," Roosevelt was to write his Secretary of War in 1944, "that every person in Germany should realize that this time Germany is a defeated nation." [7]

Detail by detail, plans for dealing with Germany were constructed so as to avoid alleged mistakes of the earlier war. Then, the Allies had asked that war criminals be punished but had left it to German courts to hear the cases, and the accused parties had all been freed or let off lightly. This time arrangements were made for their trial by the victors. Then, the Allies had stipulated that the general staff be disbanded and the armed forces kept at low levels, and the Germans had circumvented these terms. Now the Allies were to break up the high command and themselves ensure Germany's demilitarization. After World War I the Allies had sought to limit Germany's capacity for war by demanding large reparations payments. The Germans had resisted, defaulted, and eventually rebuilt their armament industries. This time the Allies were to dismantle factories and themselves determine the character and level of German industrial output. Although Roosevelt's advisers disagreed about the extent to which Germany was to be de-industrialized, no one disputed the principle. The guideline throughout was to do to Germany what the Allies of World War I had failed to do.

With regard to Japan, the previous war provided no comparable guideline, for Japan had then been an ally. Planning for defeat of Japan therefore borrowed from planning for Germany. It provided that the Japanese be made to feel their defeat, war criminals be tried by the victors, the military establishment be broken up, and industry be limited. Until the very last stages of the war, the most intensive planning centered not on Japan proper but on the Western Pacific. As a result of

World War I, the Japanese had gained control of formerly German island groups north of the equator—the Pelews, Marianas, Carolines, and Marshalls. These islands had served as bases for the Japanese Pacific offensive. Men in the American government concerned with Asia and the Pacific developed a conviction that the United States should control these islands, and from 1943 to 1945 the bulk of their thought and effort went into a campaign which had as its result the designation of these and other Pacific islands as an American strategic trusteeship under the United Nations.[8] The American government thus made ready to deal with the Japanese threat of the 1930's.

During World War II an enormous amount of labor went into preparing for the economic future. Its chief products were the International Monetary Fund and the World Bank. Their seeming importance at the time is suggested by the fact that the United States pledged to them almost six billion dollars—a sum equal to two-thirds of the last peace-time federal budget. The rationale was that economic nationalism, the hoarding of currencies, and barriers to investment and trade had led to the Great Depression; the Depression in turn had given impetus to Japanese militarism, Italian Fascism, and German Nazism; and World War II had ensued. The IMF and the World Bank together with liberalized trade arrangements were supposed to prevent recurrence of these events.

Sir Roy Harrod, biographer of the principal British delegate, Lord Keynes, has since commented that the negotiators prepared altogether for deflation such as that of 1919–21 and not at all for inflation such as actually came. Economic historian Walt Rostow writes, "They looked for the most part backward rather than forward, seeking to avoid the errors made after 1918 as these errors were subsequently understood." And Richard N. Gardner, author of the standard history of the negotiations, comments, "It is difficult to over-estimate the influence exerted by . . . 'lessons' from the past." [9]

The effort that ended in the organization of the United Nations was similarly backward-looking. Believing that the League of Nations might have blocked World War II if it had functioned according to Wilson's plans and hopes, most Americans adopted the view that the United States had been wrong not to take part. It followed that a new League should be constructed with the United States as an active participant.

Although Roosevelt had once been a staunch Wilsonian, he himself doubted that any international debating society could or would safeguard peace. Like columnist Walter Lippmann, he felt that the great mistake after World War I had been the failure of the great powers to maintain an enduring anti-German alliance.[10] Responding to bureaucratic, congressional, and public enthusiasm, Roosevelt nevertheless sponsored creation of the United Nations. In doing so he took pains to avoid what he believed to have been Wilson's tactical errors.

As Roosevelt and others saw it, Wilson had made three mistakes. He had failed to involve the Senate in drafting the Covenant. He had antagonized the Republicans and made the League a party issue. And he had banked on post-war continuation of war-time idealism. In all three respects, Roosevelt sought to do exactly the opposite.

The President consulted Senators at every stage. First, he worked with Tom Connally and other Democrats on the Foreign Relations Committee. A little later he drew in "internationalist" Republicans such as Warren Austin of Vermont and Wallace H. White of Maine. As plans began to jell, he involved the entire committee. He insisted that Secretary of State Cordell Hull exhibit to its members draft plans, alternative drafts, descriptions of plans rejected, and papers explaining why certain words and clauses were preferred to others. All this preceded any but sketchy exchanges with other governments.

Members of the Senate received full reports on the formal international discussions in 1944 at Dumbarton Oaks. When Stalin at Yalta proved unbudging in a demand for General Assembly seats for the Ukraine and Byelorussia, Roosevelt

agreed only on condition that the United States, too, be entitled
to three seats. This, he felt, would at least mollify the Senate.
Upon returning to Washington, he at once consulted Connally
and the senior Republican on the Foreign Relations Committee,
Arthur H. Vandenberg. For practical purposes he permitted
Connally and Vandenberg to decide the final American position, which turned out to be acquiescence to Stalin's demand,
coupled with reproof in the form of a public renunciation of
extra places for the United States.

Trying step by step to stay out of Woodrow Wilson's foot-
marks, Roosevelt insisted that Connally and Vandenberg be
members of the delegation to the final San Francisco conference. He plainly had his mind set on ensuring the senatorial
involvement that Wilson had failed to obtain in 1918–19.

Equally intent that the United Nations not become an elec-
toral issue, Roosevelt worked for broad Republican backing.
After Republican leaders meeting at Mackinac, Michigan,
cautiously endorsed the idea of a world organization, Roosevelt
insisted that administration plans conform with the Mackinac
resolution. The League, he remarked at a press conference,
"got dreadfully involved in American politics, instead of being
regarded as a nonpartisan subject." [11] During the presidential
campaign of 1944, he set out to forestall debate like that of
Wilson's time. To that end, he arranged for Hull to keep in
touch with his opponent's chief foreign policy adviser, John
Foster Dulles. Toward November, it is true, Roosevelt began
to charge that a Republican victory would spell a return to
isolationism. Even so, he avoided Wilson's presumed error of
claiming that votes against Democrats would be votes against
international co-operation.

Applying a further lesson from Wilson's experience, Roosevelt tried to take account of possible inconstancy on the part of
the public. He saw Wilson's frustration as due in part to false
expectations, with the final crossing of his plans accomplished
not by the Senate but by the American people and their seven

million-vote majority for Harding and "normalcy" in the election of 1920. By co-opting Senators and Republican leaders, Roosevelt might get American membership in a world organization. He interpreted history as saying, however, that the achievement would amount to little if it depended on Americans remaining internationally-minded and willing to make sacrifices for world peace.

Determined to be more realistic than Wilson, Roosevelt wanted the new organization so constructed as to survive even if American public opinion turned isolationist. His original notion, insofar as it can be discerned, involved a federation of regional organizations, with the United States responsible for peace in the Western hemisphere but not necessarily committed to act elsewhere. He spoke of the United States, Britain, Russia, and China acting as "the four policemen." When campaigning in 1944, he explained his concept with the following figure of speech:

> The Council of the United Nations must have the power to act quickly and decisively to keep the peace by force, if necessary. A policeman would not be a very effective policeman if, when he saw a felon break into a house, he had to go to the Town hall and call a town meeting before the felon could be arrested. . . .
>
> If we do not catch the international felon when we have our hands on him, if we let him get away with his loot because the Town Council has not passed an ordinance authorizing his arrest, then we are not doing our share to prevent another World War.[12]

As on other occasions, Roosevelt's words were concrete, understandable, and tantalizingly imprecise. They implied, however, that each great power might use force within its sphere without prior consent from others. If so, Congress and the public could continue to approve American membership in the United Nations even if they reverted to opposing American entanglement in European or Asian affairs or European involvement in affairs in the Western hemisphere.

In dealing with the Soviet Union, Roosevelt tried to be, or at least to appear, conciliatory. Critics later termed his behavior "appeasement." During the darker years of the Cold War, even his admirers applied the adjectives "over-optimistic" or "naïve." Roosevelt agreed to the Soviet Union's retaining the Baltic States and the territory taken from Finland, suggesting to Stalin only that these annexations be confirmed by plebiscites. He also agreed to Soviet retention of that part of Poland annexed in 1939. As for the independent nations of Eastern Europe, Roosevelt was no less insistent than Stalin that their governments be friendly to the Soviet Union. And he went out of his way to offer the Soviet Union fulfillment of what were believed to be historic Russian ambitions—free access to the Mediterranean and a warm water port in the Pacific.

Many factors led Roosevelt to act so. Immediate military concerns were certainly among them. The campaign against Hitler depended so much on Soviet soldiers that until 1945 it was hard for any American to contemplate a breach. Even then, there remained the war in the Pacific and the million casualties that Soviet intervention was supposed to prevent. Domestically, Roosevelt had to reckon in his own party with a left wing friendly to Russia. Also, he himself had some impressions which in retrospect seem to have been illusions. Like Chamberlain coming away from meeting Hitler at Berchtesgaden, Roosevelt left Teheran in 1943 feeling that Stalin was a man with whom one could do business. In 1944 he saw the Red Army stand by as Germans massacred non-communist Polish partisans. Meanwhile, the Soviet government organized its own regime for Poland. These events dismayed Roosevelt. Yet he turned away pleas for a protest, telling one Polish-American dignitary that to do so might lead to World War III with Russia. Moreover, he continued to trust the Soviet dictator. According to Harry Hopkins, the President worried lest Stalin fall and some less amiable man take his place.[13]

As with "unconditional surrender," the IMF, the World

Bank, and the United Nations, however, Roosevelt's handling of Soviet affairs can only be understood if one bears in mind his assumption that the future would be like the past. In his State of the Union message of 1944, Roosevelt justified traveling to confer with Churchill and Stalin by saying, "In the last war such discussion, such meetings, did not even begin until the shooting had stopped and the delegates began to assemble at the peace table. There had been no previous opportunities for man-to-man discussions which lead to meetings of minds. The result was a peace which was not a peace." Referring indirectly to Poland, the Soviet claim to three votes in the United Nations, and other such matters, Roosevelt also said, "Perfectionism, no less than isolationism or imperialism or power politics, may obstruct the paths to international peace. Let us not forget that the retreat to isolationism a quarter of a century ago was started not by a direct attack against international cooperation but against the alleged imperfections of the peace." [14]

Expecting the German problem to be as central after this war as after the last, Roosevelt deemed it imperative for future peace that the United States and the Soviet Union stay together. He probably thought the relationship between himself and Stalin analogous to that between Wilson and French premier Georges Clemenceau. The Paris negotiations of 1919 became rancorous in part because Wilson and other Americans had failed to understand France's intense concern for security. Having lived in peril from its birth, the communist U.S.S.R. could be seen as having at least as much reason for anxiety as the Third Republic. Roosevelt probably felt that he should show the sympathy for Stalin's point of view which Wilson had not shown for Clemenceau's, and if possible prevent the Soviet Union from turning to the sullen pre-occupation with self of Poincaré's France.

Influencing both Roosevelt's caution concerning the United Nations and his conciliation of Stalin was his apparent expectation that trends in American public opinion after World War II would parallel trends after World War I. He had seen the strength of isolationism and pacifism in Congress and among the American public in the 1930's. His proposal in 1934 that the United States join the World Court had been rejected. Congress had passed stronger neutrality laws than he desired. Even after the fall of France, he encountered strong opposition to aiding Britain, and as late as 1941 the House of Representatives almost halted the drafting of men for military service. He assumed that once peace came, isolationism and pacifism would reassert themselves irresistibly.

Roosevelt evidenced this expectation most clearly when he said to Churchill and Stalin at Yalta that the United States would probably not maintain military forces in Europe for more than two years after the war.[15] He could have made this incautious and inaccurate prediction, of course, because he bore in mind that Hiram Johnson, one of the "Irreconcilables" of 1919, remained a senior member of the Senate Foreign Relations Committee; that the sponsor of the neutrality laws, Senator Gerald Nye, was still around; that Robert A. Taft of Ohio, a last-ditch opponent of Lend-Lease, had been runner-up for the 1944 Republican presidential nomination; and that newspapers in the Hearst and Gannett chains, Mrs. Patterson's *Washington Times Herald* and *New York Daily News,* and Colonel McCormick's *Chicago Tribune* expressed views similar to those of Johnson, Nye, and Taft and reached tens of millions of readers. Counting heads, Roosevelt could have reckoned that Congress might vote to pull out of Europe. Also, Roosevelt himself may have wanted early withdrawal. In a private meeting with his chiefs of staff he once remarked, "We should not get roped into accepting any European spheres of influence." [16] Still, what seems most probable is that Roosevelt predicted early withdrawal from Europe and hedged everything else he said about post-war American commitments in large part because of a simple assumption that the future would run just as had the immediate past.

It is, of course, understandable that Roosevelt and his associates should have drawn on history when estimating the future and planning for it. What is surprising is how completely their post-war planning was controlled by a handful of analogies and parallels, all from their own lifetime. Had Roosevelt or some of his advisers considered the Napoleonic wars as an alternative historical example, they might have foreseen the possibility that Germany, like Restoration France, might be a weak force for a long period and that meetings of the United Nations might resemble the congresses of Aix, Troppau, Laibach, and Verona, vexing rather than composing relations among the great powers. Remembering Tsar Alexander I, they might have envisioned a possible effort by Stalin to dominate Central and Eastern Europe and extend Russian influence into Western Europe, the Mediterranean, Asia, and even the Western hemisphere.

Although developments after World War II were in fact to be more like those after the Napoleonic Wars than those after World War I, there is no reason why Roosevelt and the men around him should necessarily have assumed this to be probable. At least some of them, however, knew something about this earlier history. Some probably had knowledge of the still earlier history of peacemaking after the Thirty Years War and the wars of Louis XIV. What seems unaccountable is that they appear never to have imagined that the pattern of events after World War II could differ significantly from that after World War I. The administration's vision of the post-war world seems to have been dominated by a single image.

Similarly, Roosevelt and his advisers appear to have assumed that American public opinion after World War II would revert to being what it had been before the war. That they adopted this assumption is also easy to understand. On the other hand, just as one may criticize them for recurring to only one historical parallel, so one may also take them to task for not recognizing that the future might not proceed in a straight line from the immediate past. In fact, if they had paused to think about the forces that had shaped public opinion earlier, they might have had reason to doubt that it would be the same after the war as before. They might have recalled, for example, that the American people had not opposed involvement in those areas of the world where the United States could be dominant—the Western hemisphere and, to an extent, East Asia. Knowing that the United States would emerge from the war as incomparably the world's greatest power, they might have foreseen the possibility that the public would no longer resist an active American role in Europe or the Middle East. Likewise, Roosevelt or some of the men around him could have recognized that the future "foreign policy public"—that portion of the public potentially interested in foreign affairs—might well include significantly more Jews and Roman Catholics, especially of Italian and Polish background, and that these groups might not exhibit the same attitudes as the English and North European Protestants and Irish Catholics who had previously predominated. Remembering, too, the fervent anti-communism which had occasionally surfaced among older as well as newer religious and ethnic groups, they might have visualized a new "Red scare" of larger proportions than that of 1919–20. It would be too much to contend that Roosevelt and his advisers should have put out of mind any fear that the post-war public would be isolationist and assumed instead that it would support large overseas commitments and become militantly anti-communist. It can be said, however, that had they been more sensitive to factors that produce discontinuities in history, they might have taken into account the possibility that the future would be what in fact it was.

None of what appears here is intended as an attack on the Roosevelt administration's actions. Its preparations for dealing with Germany and Japan, efforts in behalf of the IMF,

the World Bank, and the United Nations, and conciliation of
the Soviet Union may well have been the best possible courses
of action. After the fact, one cannot easily assert that different
courses would have had happier outcomes, for one only knows
what happened, not what would have happened had a whole
sequence of events been given a different turn. There is a
wholesome truth in Lord Halifax's response to the question of
whether he regretted the Munich agreement. "Oh well," he
said, "if you don't make one mistake, you make another." [17]

What can properly be criticized is the superficial reasoning
that produced the Roosevelt administration's policies. The
records indicate that the President and his advisers were cap-
tivated by a single conception of the future, based largely on
their beliefs about the recent past. It is not unreasonable to
say that they should have considered alternative shapes which
the future might take and at least speculated about a world
in which, among other things, Germany and Japan were impotent, inflation persisted, and the American public became
wedded to the idea that the United States bore responsibility
for maintaining peace and order in the world. The fact appears to be that, like generals preparing for the last war,
American statesmen of World War II thought only in terms
of the last post-war era.

II

The Cold War:
Preventing World War II

World War II was swiftly followed by the Cold War. For this
turn of events, many explanations have been offered. For a
long time, most Americans took it for granted that the United
States had simply responded to aggressive expansionist moves
by a Soviet government bent on forcing communism upon the
world. Later, as tension eased, many began to pay more attention to "revisionists" who contended that in actuality the
United States had brought on the Cold War by attempting
to impose democracy and capitalism upon countries adjoin-
ing Russia, threatening thus to create a new *cordon sanitaire*,
and provoking defensive moves by Stalin.

Although it can hardly be said that the "revisionists" have
proved their case, they have established that there is no quick
and simple answer to the question of why and how American
leaders so rapidly adopted the view that Russia, the war-time
ally, should be regarded, and responded to, as a dangerous
enemy. Since hitherto sealed American documents of the early
post-war period have just been opened, moreover, it has become possible to speculate about this question on the basis
of somewhat more evidence than was previously available.

A hypothesis first popularized by the "revisionist" writer, Gar Alperovitz, is that the American government was taken over by men who were ideologically anti-Soviet. Roosevelt died in April 1945. Vice President Harry S Truman, who succeeded him, was a former Missouri Senator with almost no background in foreign affairs. As Alperovitz notes, he had nevertheless given voice to a strong prejudice against communism. After Hitler's invasion of Russia in 1941, he had publicly expressed hope that the Nazis and communists would kill one another off.[1]

Since Roosevelt himself had largely managed war-time relations with the U.S.S.R., the men committed to conciliating the Russians were for the most part members of his staff, friends, or protégés. Naturally, these were the first people to leave office or to be replaced by Truman. Harry Hopkins was used by the new President for one special mission to Moscow, partly to reassure Stalin and partly to seek seats for non-communists in the cabinet which the Russians had set up in Poland. Hopkins, however, did not develop a close relationship with Truman. In any case, he was sick most of the time and died not long after the end of the war. Secretary of the Treasury Henry Morgenthau lost his easy access to the White House, became petulant, and was soon allowed to retire. Truman retained Fleet Admiral William D. Leahy as Chief of Staff to the Commander-in-Chief and liaison with the Joint Chiefs of Staff, and he appointed as Secretary of State James F. Byrnes, who had been Roosevelt's "assistant President" in charge of war mobilization and had been present at Yalta. Neither Leahy nor Byrnes, however, had a personal stake in Roosevelt's post-war planning. Of men who did, only Secretary of Commerce Henry A. Wallace remained at a high level in the new administration.

Most of Truman's chosen advisers were men more or less on the right wing of the Democratic party. Aware that Byrnes would spend much of his time at international conferences, Truman expected to receive information and advice chiefly through the Under Secretary of State. For that post, he chose Dean Acheson, a Washington lawyer who had been in the Treasury department in the first Roosevelt administration but resigned because of disapproval of Roosevelt's financial expedients. In the defense establishment, Truman retained and came to rely upon Secretary of the Navy James V. Forrestal. As both a Roman Catholic and a former investment banker, Forrestal was strongly anti-communist. At least as early as May 1945 he observed to a friend that Soviet communism was "as incompatible with democracy as was Nazism or Fascism," and he was continually on the lookout for material proving that this was the case.[2] There can be little doubt that Truman and most of his advisers were less disposed than their predecessors to be tolerant of the Soviet Union.

On the other hand, it is not at all evident that these men started out with an assumption that the Soviet Union was an enemy and should be approached as such. When speaking in 1941, Truman had merely voiced an attitude widely held by Americans throughout the period of the Nazi-Soviet alliance. Scarcely three months afterward, he voted for extending lend-lease aid to Russia.[3] When he suddenly became President, he found debate in progress between Washington and Moscow over certain issues relating to the forthcoming conference on the United Nations Charter. Believing the Russians to be reneging on agreements made with Roosevelt at Yalta, he gave Soviet Foreign Minister Vyacheslav Molotov a verbal dressing down which led the Russian to exclaim, "I have never been talked to like that in my life."[4] Within a matter of weeks, however, when Truman dispatched Hopkins to Moscow, he commissioned him to reassure Stalin that the United States would keep any and all of Roosevelt's pledges. At the same time, he enlisted veteran Russophile Joseph E. Davies as a special emissary to Churchill in London. Most of what Truman said in 1945 and even in 1946 indicated both hope and belief that American-Soviet differences would be accommodated.

While the majority of advisers selected by Truman were relatively conservative men, few were ideologues. Byrnes had no doctrinaire convictions. He was chiefly an artful compromiser. Though Acheson had parted company with Roosevelt over monetary policy, he had remained a loyal Democrat. During the war he had returned to federal service as an Assistant Secretary of State. In that post he had managed to remain on good terms with members of most of the department's internal factions. Journalists of both Russophobe and Russophile leanings judged him open-minded and applauded his selection as Under Secretary.[5] If Forrestal was manifestly anti-Soviet, his colleague, Secretary of War Henry L. Stimson, was not. On the contrary, Stimson insisted on the need for enduring American-Soviet co-operation. Though Truman and his advisers differed somewhat from their predecessors in attitudes toward communism and the Soviet Union, their prejudices and predispositions can serve as only one small element in explanation of why American policy altered so rapidly at the close of World War II.

More important was the fact that Truman and the men around him received much of their tutoring about foreign affairs from diplomats who deliberately sought to teach them that the Soviet Union was malevolent and untrustworthy. Roosevelt had had little to do with these diplomats. With some justice, he had judged professionals in the State Department to be Republicans at heart, unsympathetic with his domestic programs, and generally critical of his initiatives in international relations. In the late 1930's he began to circumvent them when dealing with European crises. Once the war commenced, he bypassed them most of the time, relying chiefly on his staff, emergency agencies, the military establishment, and the Treasury for information and advice about all matters except the construction of new international organizations. Truman, on the other hand, assumed office with the conventional view that the State Department was and should be the principal organization dealing with foreign affairs. When he took over the oval office, the department's professionals for the first time in years found themselves filing reports and memoranda with a prospect of significantly affecting what a President thought, said, and did.

During the war, these professionals had looked on impotently while relations with the Soviet Union were managed by men whom they judged naïve at best. Hopkins reportedly quoted Roosevelt as saying of Stalin, "if I give him everything I possibly can and ask nothing from him in return, *noblesse oblige,* he won't try to annex anything and will work with me for a world of democracy and peace." And Morgenthau, wholly on the basis of negotiating with them at Bretton Woods, pronounced the Soviets "intelligent and reasonable." [6] The State Department's professionals regarded such views as utterly mistaken.

The diplomats had formed their opinions through prolonged observation of Soviet conduct. Joseph C. Grew, the dean of American Foreign Service officers, was Under Secretary of State when Truman became President. Although near retirement age and soon replaced by Acheson, he may have been typical of the careerists who advised the administration. After World War I he had had the assignment of reporting from Denmark on what could be learned of the Bolsheviks in Russia. Everything about them repelled him. Above all, he found their resort to propaganda and subversion instead of diplomacy repugnant. Nor was his opinion improved by face to face negotiations with Russian Foreign Minister Boris Chicherin at Lausanne in 1922–23. In his diary Grew described the fussy, scholarly, and somewhat effeminate Chicherin as "a Bolshevik bird of prey, with malignant eyes and a beak nose." When the Roosevelt administration extended recognition to the Soviet Union, Grew, then ambassador to Japan, regarded the action as a mistake. He also deplored his government's condemnation of Japan's seizure of Manchuria, one reason being that he saw Japan as a "staunch buffer" against the spread of communism. While regretting Hitler's take-over in Germany, he thought at first that the Germans had at least been spared the worse evil of turning communist. Although he later came to think the Nazis just as bad, the Nazi-Soviet pact and the Russo-Finnish war confirmed his belief that the two systems were congeners.[7] The later war-time partnership did not alter his opinion in the least. In May 1945 he put on paper reflections that drew upon his prolonged, if second-hand, observation of Soviet behavior. The war's result, he wrote, "will be merely the transfer of totalitarian dictatorship from Germany and Japan to Soviet Russia which will constitute in future as grave a danger to us as did the Axis." Taking it as given that Russia would control the states on her European border, he continued:

> With her certain stranglehold on these countries, Russia's power will steadily increase and she will in the not distant future be in a favorable position to expand her control, step by step, through Europe. . . .
> A future war with Soviet Russia is as certain as anything in the world can be certain. . . .
> The most fatal thing we can do is to place any confidence whatever in Russia's sincerity, knowing without question that she will take every opportunity to profit by our clinging to our own ethical international standards. She regards and will continue to regard our ethical behavior as a weakness to us and an asset to her.[8]

Next below Grew in the State Department hierarchy, and remaining in his post after Byrnes and Acheson took over, was James Clement Dunn. As Assistant Secretary for European, Asian, Near Eastern, and African Affairs, he screened all diplomatic reportage except that from Latin America. During the

1930's, Dunn had clearly regarded a victory in Spain by the Italian- and German-backed Nationalists as preferable to a victory by the Soviet-backed Republicans, and in 1941 he had seen the German attack on Russia as possibly ending in German victory and thus creating opportunity for the United States to undo the mistake of extending recognition to the Soviet regime.[9] It seems plausible that he felt as much antipathy for the Soviet Union as did Grew.

Under Dunn were the directors of three regional offices, those for Europe, the Far East, and the Near East and Africa. Heading the European office was H. Freeman Matthews. Nicknamed "Doc" because of post-graduate work at the École des Sciences Politiques, he had served in Paris from 1937 to 1939 under William C. Bullitt, who, as Beatrice Farnsworth comments, had an "obsessive fear of the Soviet Union." At the time of his appointment to man the European desk, the left-wing journal *PM* assessed him as "rather on the conservative side but by no means a reactionary"; as late as the winter of 1945 Russian specialist George Kennan regarded him as somewhat innocent about the Soviets. If so, Matthews proved a quick learner, for he was soon writing that "the U.S. must accept the fact that it is confronted with the threat of an expanding totalitarian state . . . [and] that this policy of expansion by direct and indirect means will be continuous and unlimited." [10]

On a level with Matthews was Loy Henderson, who headed the Office of Near Eastern and African Affairs, taking in Greece, Turkey, and Iran. The most senior of Foreign Service Soviet specialists, he had sided with Bullitt in 1941 in a bureaucratic battle to prevent appointment of a Hopkins protégé to handle lend-lease aid to Russia. After losing, he had been taken off the Soviet desk and on White House orders shifted to dealing with non-Russian affairs. It remained his conviction that higher officials in the department and the government did not understand the strength of Soviet hatred for capitalist states and the unscrupulousness and untrustworthiness of the communist leaders.[11]

Men with views similar to those of Grew, Dunn, Matthews, and Henderson filed the reports from the field which Washington desk officers winnowed. Since ambassadorships to war-devastated capitals hardly seemed ripe patronage plums, career Foreign Service officers occupied many of the key embassies. There were some exceptions, notably in Moscow, where the chief U.S. representative was W. Averell Harriman, a former banker and railroad executive, a New Deal administrator, a friend of Roosevelt and Hopkins, and a man often used for missions requiring blunt speech and close bargaining; and Yugoslavia, where the ambassador was former RKO board chairman Richard C. Patterson, a diplomatic novice. But even the non-professionals were aided by Foreign Service assistants. Harriman had George Kennan as his principal deputy, and Patterson was guided by Harold Shantz, a twenty-three-year veteran who had served under Bullitt in Moscow in 1934–36 and had been in Finland during the Soviet-Finnish war.

The other American ambassadors around the western and southwestern rim of the Soviet Union were for the most part career men. Arthur Bliss Lane, the ambassador to Poland, had served in Warsaw during the Soviet-Polish war of 1919 and been in the Baltic states and Yugoslavia in 1936–41. He yielded to no one in his distrust of the U.S.S.R.[12] Maynard B. Barnes, the ambassador to Bulgaria, had been first secretary in Paris under Bullitt and "Doc" Matthews, and Edwin C. Wilson, the ambassador to Turkey, had worked as Bullitt's counselor. Although little is on record to show the previous attitudes toward the Soviet Union of Barnes, Wilson, or Burton Y. Berry, the ambassador to Rumania, or Wallace Murray and George Allen, the successive ambassadors to Iran, their dispatches demonstrated that they shared the inclinations of the officers to whom they reported in Washington. To a man, these professionals wanted to communicate to the political leaders above them an understanding that the Soviet Union and the international communist movement were hostile forces.

Some did so straightforwardly. Kennan's dispatches from Moscow were models. Writing gracefully and learnedly, he set forth his own forceful judgments about long-term trends in Russian and Soviet behavior. He warned, for example, "There is nothing—I repeat nothing—in the history of the Soviet regime which could justify us in assuming that the men who are now in power in Russia . . . would hesitate for a moment to apply their power against us if by doing so they thought that they might materially improve their own power position in the world." Also, he declared, "The endless, fluid pursuit of power is a habit of Russian statesmanship, ingrained not only in the traditions of the Russian State but also in the ideology of the Communist Party." [13]

Much reportage by diplomats, however, was tendentious. Ambassador Wilson once commented that he could not take much reassurance from ratification of the United Nations treaty by a power that had signed the Nazi-Soviet pact, and Barnes spoke in a dispatch from Sofia of the Russian "record for double dealing." [14] Despite his relative ignorance of Soviet affairs, Matthews wrote as if he had as much expertise as Kennan, saying, for example, that "it can be stated on the basis of experience that Soviet suspicion of the motives of other countries is a deliberately artificial thesis spread by the Soviet Government primarily for internal reasons, but for consumption both at home and abroad, and not a conclusion reached by an objective and honest evaluation of the actions of other countries." [15] Though Kennan's generalizations had the same import and were put with more force, they were cast in a form open to challenge by another authority on Russia. Those of Wilson, Barnes, and Matthews had more the quality one associates with Soviet statements that commence "*kak izvestnyi*"—"as is well known."

Some diplomats misrepresented or at least oversimplified the background of issues with the U.S.S.R. Barnes's reportage from Sofia serves as an example; for the overthrow and murder of Aleksandr Stamboliski in 1923 had been followed by what even so cautious a source as *The Encyclopedia Britannica* describes as a long period of "repressive measures more fitted for emergencies than for normal times," succeeded during the Great Depression by a more "authoritarian trend" and "a semi-dictatorial government" and after 1940 by a pro-German government under Bogdan Filov, which preserved neutrality, "fearing a revolt of the predominantly pro-Russian masses." The leading historical survey, *The Balkans in Our Time* by Robert Lee Wolff, asserts that "Bulgarian political life was a mess. Bulgaria reached the period of the Second World War under a tight police dictatorship." [16]

Barnes had some knowledge of recent Bulgarian history. He had served in the country in 1930–34, and he once sent a private letter to Matthews reflecting considerable grasp of what had happened before and later. Writing in April 1945, Barnes commented, "As I see matters here, we are now going through the 1944 Bulgarian version of what began to happen to Russia in November 1917; or, to put it another way, September 9, 1944, in Bulgaria picked up the threads of the Stambolisky regime, broken by the coup d'état of June 1923." [17]

In dispatches likely to be passed up the line to the Secretary of State or the President, however, Barnes painted a monochromatic background. He characterized Bulgaria's notoriously corrupt Agrarian party as enthusiastically supported by 60 per cent of the peasantry. His cables implied that the only period of authoritarian rule in Bulgaria had been that of war-time collaboration with the Nazis. The communists, he contended, were seeking to turn Bulgaria over to Russia just as Filov had turned it over to Germany. Their opponents he described as "those who still hope for the *re-establishment* of civil and human liberties." [18] Whether designedly or not, Barnes conveyed the misleading impression that Soviet-backed communists had imposed a dictatorship on a country which had been and otherwise would be democratic.

Berry did likewise in communications from Rumania. His cables spoke of democratic forces that would *re-emerge* if not suppressed by the communists. When Kentucky publisher Mark Ethridge toured Eastern Europe in 1945 as a special agent of President Truman, Berry coached him to write of the old Peasant party leader, Julius Maniu, as "the unquestionable symbol of Rumanian democracy and of traditionally Rumanian and democratic feeling." [19] Like Barnes, Berry sketched a background which much overstated the historic power of democratic forces in the Balkans.

Few competing assessments reached Truman. During the war, an Office of Strategic Services, nominally under the Joint Chiefs of Staff, had gathered intelligence abroad and also maintained in Washington a large research and analysis organization manned by scholars with deep knowledge of foreign areas. With the end of the war, however, the O.S.S. practically ceased to function. Many of its officers hurried back to private life. In any case, the President, as he records in his memoirs, found it irritating that reports came across his desk "on the same subject at different times from the various departments, and these reports often conflicted." [20] Hence he directed that all assessment of intelligence be centralized in State. In fact, senior Foreign Service officers were to resist absorbing the O.S.S., and Truman, somewhat against his will, felt compelled eventually to create an independent Central Intelligence Agency.[21] Meanwhile, for practical purposes, he denied himself any political intelligence except that which filtered through State.

The one source of information and advice other than the State Department was the military establishment. By closing down the White House map room, Truman cut himself off from continuous access to traffic over military communication lines. In other ways, he put some distance between himself and the Pentagon, making it clear that he would rely on the military much less heavily than had Roosevelt. Nevertheless, the involvement in political affairs of overseas commands, the Joint Chiefs, and the secretaries of War and the Navy had become sufficiently routinized so that cables and memoranda from military sources inevitably came to the President's desk.

In short order, however, men in the military establishment adopted and began to parrot State Department estimates of the Soviet Union and of potential American-Soviet issues. Secretary of the Navy James Forrestal circulated and advertised Kennan's analyses. Naval officers and airmen soon recognized that, if the distant and immense U.S.S.R. were perceived as an enemy, it would be much easier to win authorization for spending on carriers and bombers. The army slowly followed suit. By early 1946 the Joint Chiefs were saying unanimously that

> —the consolidation and development of the power of Russia is the greatest threat to the United States in the foreseeable future. . . . United States foreign policy should continually give consideration to our immediate capabilities for supporting our policy by arms if the occasion should demand, rather than to our long term potential, which, owing to the length of time required for mobilization of the nation's resources, might not be sufficient to avert disaster in another war.[22]

On the whole, the bureaucracy presented to Truman and his advisers a picture of a powerful, ambitious, ruthless, and deceitful Soviet Union. Of course, the diplomats did not imagine or invent all that they reported. Communists in East European countries did employ ruthless tactics against their opponents, and Soviet authorities lent them all kinds of aid. Nevertheless, it seems clear now that many of the diplomats indulged in overstatement, probably in order to counteract the excessive trustfulness and optimism which they had earlier observed among politicians. Some of them used black and white to portray issues that might have been sketched more faithfully in grays.

Given the predispositions of members of the Truman administration, the diplomats' reports were probably read with less skepticism than would have been the case had Roosevelt and his circle remained in office. This is not necessarily to accuse Truman and the men around him of gullibility. The President was aware that a number of professional diplomats were strongly anti-Soviet. He acknowledged the fact when talking with Joseph Davies in May 1945. Moreover, he came soon to share his predecessor's relatively low opinion of the State Department.[23] Similarly, Byrnes did not wholly trust the men who worked for him. In fact, when seeking to negotiate compromises with the Russians, he tried to keep his activities secret from the department.[24] Acheson, Forrestal, and others in the administration were men of extraordinary intelligence and sophistication, not easily to be taken in by biased reportage. Nevertheless, it seems likely that the diplomats' dispatches, coming in day after day, not offset by other sources, and with their essential message echoed and re-echoed in memoranda from State Department and military officers, eventually produced some of their intended effect. In other words, one must explain the turn in American official attitudes toward the Soviet Union in small part by the prejudices of U.S. leaders, in larger part by occurrences in Europe and the Middle East, and in perhaps still larger part by the manner in which those occurrences were described and interpreted by the American bureaucracy.

Still, however, the explanation remains insufficient. For Truman and his associates did not just become antipathetic toward the Soviet Union; they adopted the position that communist Russia represented a threat which the United States had to resist, if necessary by war. They could have seen the developments reported by the diplomats as at most cause for public expressions of regret. In the preceding decade, American officials had so viewed Fascist or Nazi take-overs in Spain, Austria, and Czechoslovakia. Why did members of the Truman administration react differently?

The most plausible answer is that they came to see the events described by their diplomats as analogous to the events of the 1930's. By then, it was generally thought that the American government had been wrong to regard the Fascist and Nazi actions as not affecting the security of the United States. World War II had been made inevitable, ran the conventional wisdom, because the Western democracies had not recognized early enough the menace to them of the expansionist drive of Fascism and had not resisted its initial manifestations. Once Truman and the men around him perceived developments of the 1940's as parallel to those of the 1930's, they applied this moral and hence resolved to behave toward the Soviet Union as they believed their predecessors should have behaved toward the expansionist states of their time.

Diplomats encouraged acceptance of this way of viewing the Soviet Union. Lane in Warsaw described communist Poland as having a government "based on a Nazi or Fascist system of police control." Berry's military collaborator, General Cortlandt Schuyler, characterized the Rumanian communists as "Russian Quislings." Borrowing a word previously applied to German-controlled states, Barnes spoke of Bulgaria as a Russian "satellite." With reference to Yugoslavia, a dispatch from Patterson also used the term "satellite," and Shantz, portraying Tito's communist government as "a ruthless totalitarian police regime," compared its internal security agency to the Gestapo. Lane once made explicit the implicit moral, writing that "Appeasement or apparent appeasement can be as dangerous to United States interests in 1945 as it actually was in 1940 or 1941." [25]

It is unlikely, however, that the diplomats' reportage had such suggestive power as to implant the analogy in the minds of the President and his associates. It seems more probable that they arrived at such a frame of reference on their own.

When coping with some of the earliest problems before them, members of the Truman administration organized their thought around analogies from the inter-war years. The clearest evidence appears in discussions of post-war control of the atomic bomb. Secretary of War Stimson, who had overseen the bomb's development, favored sharing the secret of how to make it with the Soviets right away. They would soon learn on their own, he argued, and a show of trust might evoke trust. In a cabinet meeting in September 1945 Forrestal opposed Stimson. As Walter Millis summarizes Forrestal's notes,

> He made the point that the bomb and the knowledge that produced it were "the property of the American people," which the administration could not give away until they were sure it was the sense of the people that they should do so. He reminded them that in World War I the Japanese had been our allies, like the Russians in World War II; that we had afterward made naval agreements with the Japanese which we had lived up to but which they had not, and that "the Russians, like the Japanese, are essentially Oriental in their thinking and until we have a longer record of experience with them on the validity of engagements . . . it seems doubtful that we should endeavor to buy their understanding and sympathy. We tried that once with Hitler. There are no returns on appeasement." [26]

Truman nevertheless directed that a proposal for international control be developed. Acheson took the assignment, enlisting help from David E. Lilienthal of the Tennessee Valley Authority. While deliberating, Acheson, Lilienthal, and their colleagues did not lose sight of the precedent cited by Forrestal. The official historians of the Atomic Energy Commission report of one session:

> Acheson drew a parallel with the Washington Disarmament Conference of 1921–22. The idea of heading off a

naval race had been a good one, but the content of the
treaties was wrong. Worse, the United States did not
build up to treaty limits and the Japanese fortified their
island bases. The present situation was much the same.[27]

Acheson and Lilienthal ended up proposing transfer to a
United Nations agency of control over known reserves of
uranium ore, all facilities for producing atomic bombs, and
most of the scientists who would work on either peaceful or
military uses of nuclear energy. They stipulated, however, that
the United States so time the transfers as to retain interim
power to use atomic weapons if any nation cheated and built
up a secret nuclear hoard.

After receiving the Acheson-Lilienthal report, Truman and
Byrnes asked Bernard M. Baruch to present the plan before
the United Nations. The domestic czar during World War I,
Baruch was old and vain. He resisted acting as a mere "mes-
senger boy." He added two features which made the plan
distinctively his own: first, condign punishment for any vio-
lator of the agreement; second and more important, that no
great power be able to veto such punishment. Reminiscing,
Baruch was to write: "The lesson of the League and the fight
over Article X of the Covenant—the record of meaningless
disarmament agreements and renunciations of war—were
very much in my mind." [28]

In the United Nations the Russians rejected the Baruch
plan. Having a start on nuclear weapons of their own and
having spies in Britain, Canada, and in the American labora-
tory at Los Alamos, they probably would have taken the same
stand even if the plan had not had the features added by
Baruch. Many besides communists made the argument, however, that the United States had asked too much of the U.S.S.R.
and offered too little. Responding to such criticism, Byrnes
declared that as a young Congressman he had endorsed the
arms limitation plans of 1920–22. "What happened thereafter

influences my thinking today," he said. "While America scrapped battleships, Japan scrapped blueprints. America will not again make that mistake." [29]

By 1946, however, members of the Truman administration were seldom citing parallels from the early inter-war period. Instead, they were moving rapidly outward to the view that the significant parallels were those after the Manchurian incident of 1931. One sees this most plainly in the evolution of their thinking about the Eastern Mediterranean and Middle East.

From the outset, State Department careerists had pictured the Soviets as threatening this region. As early as March 1945 the mission in Ankara reported that the Russians intended to take control of Turkey. At the time of Truman's meeting with Stalin at Potsdam, the ambassador in Teheran quoted the young Shah as saying that Russia had designs on Iran and that its tactics were reminiscent of Nazi Germany's. In August Henderson's division prepared a memorandum for the President arguing that the Soviets would move into the whole Middle East if the United States did not actively block them.[30]

Despite the reportage from Eastern Europe coming to his desk, Truman still seemed to feel that issues with the Russians could be ironed out. In November, Henderson arranged for a meeting between the President and several diplomats home on leave from Middle Eastern posts. Referring to the Arab princes, one of the diplomats said, "If the United States fails them, they will turn to Russia and will be lost to our civilization." According to Henderson's notes, "the President said that he would like these countries to turn toward both Russia and the United States." [31] During the same period, Truman encouraged planning for international control of nuclear weapons, and Byrnes did his best to find formulas that could break the deadlock with the Soviets on peace terms for Europe and

Asia. In Kennan's scornful view, Byrnes's main purpose was "to achieve some sort of agreement, he doesn't much care what." [32]

Messages coming through Henderson's division continued to warn of Russian designs. From Greece, where armed conflict seemed likely to resume at any time between the government and the communist-led opposition, a dispatch reported the commander of British occupation forces as declaring that if the United States and Britain did not jointly support the government, a "Red Tide" would roll across the country. From Turkey, cables continued to predict Soviet efforts to acquire ascendancy, perhaps even by armed conquest. From Iran came reports that Russian occupation forces were not preparing to evacuate the northern province of Azerbaijan, as provided for in war-time agreements, but were rather organizing their own regime and preventing access by forces or agents of the Iranian government. In Washington, the Iranian ambassador pleaded for American support, saying that Azerbaijan "was only first move in a series which would include Turkey and other countries in Near East." If the province were not denied to the Russians, he declared, the "history of Manchuria, Abyssinia, and Munich would be repeated and Azerbaijan would prove to have been first shot fired in third world war." [33]

Taking much the same line, Henderson argued that the most important interest of the United States in the region was to prevent "developments . . . which might make a mockery of the principles on which the United Nations Organization rests . . . and which might eventually give birth to a Third World War." Describing the Soviet Union as determined to expand "across Turkey and through the Dardanelles into the Mediterranean, and across Iran and through the Persian Gulf into the Indian Ocean," he contended that the United States ought to arrest its progress before World War III became inevitable.[34]

The President ultimately accepted this advice. Early in 1946 he drafted a longhand letter to Byrnes. Whether he delivered it is a matter of dispute. In any case, he set forth his opinions. The Ethridge report convinced him, he said, that Bulgaria and Rumania were "police states." Soviet conduct in Poland was "high-handed and arbitrary." He dwelt particularly on Iran—"Another outrage if I ever saw one." He continued, "There isn't a doubt in my mind that Russia intends an invasion of Turkey and the seizure of the Black Sea Straits to the Mediterranean. Unless Russia is faced with an iron fist and strong language another war is in the making." [35]

When the fixed date for Soviet withdrawal from Iran arrived, with Russian troops still in Azerbaijan, Truman decided to protest to Moscow and to second Iran's formally bringing the matter before the United Nations.

As it turned out, the Iranian prime minister negotiated an agreement with the Russians. Soviet troops pulled out, leaving a pro-Soviet regime in Azerbaijan, and the Iranian government in return agreed that a joint Soviet-Iranian company should have oil drilling rights in northern Iran. Even at the time, some suspicion arose that the oil deal might have been the preoccupation of both parties, with the Russians holding up troop withdrawal in order to press the Iranians into signing, and the Iranians enlisting the United States and the United Nations in hope of beating down the Russian terms. There also seemed grounds for suspecting that the prime minister and the Shah, when dealing with Moscow and Washington, were less concerned with either the integrity of the northern provinces or oil than with their own duel for control of the parliament in Teheran.[36] In retrospect, these hypotheses seem even more plausible. The President, the Secretary of State, and others in the administration, however, saw only that the United States had been firm and that the Soviets had backed down.

Not long afterward, the administration was advised that it

faced another and more serious test. In early August 1946
the Soviet government proposed that, instead of Turkey alone
controlling the Turkish straits, there be established "a regime
. . . under the competence of Turkey and other Black Sea
powers." In addition, Moscow proposed that Turkey and the
U.S.S.R. "organize joint means of defense of the Straits." Although Turkish officials took the Soviet démarche calmly,
Ambassador Wilson did not. He cabled from Ankara that the
U.S.S.R. was "seeking make use Straits question in order destroy Turkish independence, establish 'friendly' regime Turkey,
thereby closing one remaining gap in chain Soviet satellite
states from Baltic to Black Sea." Wilson continued, "Turkish
independence has become vital interest U.S. If Turkey falls
under Soviet control last barrier removed in way Soviet advance to Persian Gulf and Suez and temptation would be
more than human nature could withstand. Once this happens
fat is in fire again." [37]

In Washington, the military establishment had long since
rallied to the position best represented by Henderson. Once
sensing possible presidential interest in the region, naval officers had been quick to suggest that a task force be sent to,
or even stationed in, the Mediterranean. After initially approving the idea, Truman had had second thoughts. He authorized only a symbolic visit by the battleship *Missouri*. Enthusiasm in the navy for a larger and more permanent mission
continued unabated.[38] Among army officers, the President's
support of Iran had awakened the thought that the United
States might provide military supplies and even possibly military training to nations in the Middle East.

When asked for a formal comment on the Soviet proposals
to Turkey, the Joint Chiefs responded forebodingly. Even nom-
inal participation in defense of the Straits, they warned, would
give the Soviet Union a bridgehead. Everyone in Turkey
would perceive that the Russians could rapidly reinforce this
bridgehead. The chiefs predicted that "this situation would so

soften the Turkish attitude toward Russia as to soon result in
reducing Turkey to a satellite Soviet state." Were this to occur,
they went on, the entire Eastern Mediterranean and Middle
East would probably be controlled by the Russians in the
event of war. Meanwhile, the self-confidence of all the nations
in the Middle East and Europe would be shaken. On the
basis of this logic, the chiefs emphatically recommended economic and military aid to Turkey, including the possible dispatch of a military advisory mission.[39]

With the embassy in Ankara, the State Department's experts, and the spokesmen for the military all of one mind, the
President's principal advisers could hardly take the situation
in Turkey lightly. At the time, Byrnes was attending a conference in Paris. Acheson acted as Secretary of State. He,
Forrestal, and Secretary of War Robert Patterson conferred
and agreed upon a document to be submitted to the President.
It declared:

> We believe that if the Soviet Union succeeds in intro-
> ducing into Turkey armed forces with the ostensible pur-
> pose of enforcing the joint control of the Straits, the Soviet
> Union will use these forces in order to obtain control
> over Turkey.
> If the Soviet Union succeeds in its objective obtain-
> ing control over Turkey it will be extremely difficult, if
> not impossible, to prevent the Soviet Union from obtaining
> control over Greece and over the whole Near and Middle
> East. . . .
> When we refer to the Near and Middle East, we have
> in mind the territory lying between the Mediterranean and
> India. When the Soviet Union has once obtained full
> mastery of this territory . . . it will be in a much stronger
> position to obtain its objectives in India and China.

Asserting thus that the fate of all the Asian continent, and
perhaps of the world, hung in the balance, the three secretaries
went on to observe that a retreat by the Soviet Union "cannot be brought about by skillful argument or the appeal to

reason. The only thing which will deter the Russians will be the conviction that the United States is prepared, if necessary, to meet aggression with force of arms." Concluding, they emphasized that "the best hope of preserving peace is that the conviction should be carried to the U.S.S.R., Turkey and all other powers that . . . the United States would not hesitate to join other nations in meeting armed aggression by the force of American arms." [40]

When the secretaries went to the White House to deliver this document, they took along the chiefs of staff. Making it clear that he understood himself to be agreeing to war should the Soviets actually attack Turkey, Truman said that he would hold the recommended posture "to the end." [41]

In this meeting, the President and his advisers agreed on what should be, as the secretaries put it, their "inner conviction." They also agreed that open threats were not yet in order. In fact, the only practical action on which they decided was a diplomatic note to Turkey, stating opposition in principle to any bilateral arrangements for the Straits. This was followed by similar notes to the United Kingdom and the Soviet Union.

The August understanding about the administration's "inner conviction" nevertheless set in train a number of changes. In Greece, the elections under American and British supervision had given a mandate to an essentially right-wing government. Moreover, a plebiscite had had the surprising result of bringing about restoration of the monarchy. Anti-government and anti-monarchist groups, with communists in the lead, reopened a civil war. As was reported to Byrnes, still in Paris, experts in Washington agreed that the Soviet agents were "undoubtedly responsible" for arming these insurgents and that their aim was "to set up in Greece a government which would be subservient to the Soviet Union." [42] In Iran, the separatist regime survived in Azerbaijan. Although the existing parliament in Teheran was anti-Soviet (and was, indeed, to refuse ratification of the oil agreement with the U.S.S.R.), the Shah and the government felt themselves under pressure to hold elections; the U.S. mission in Iran agreed with the Shah that elections would probably bring in a parliament disposed to make accommodations with the Soviet Union. The experts in Washington were unanimous in believing that the eventual outcome would be a Soviet-dominated Iran.[43] The Near Eastern division of State and the Joint Chiefs joined in pressing for economic and especially military aid not only to Turkey but also to Greece and Iran.

Although Truman prided himself on being able to make a decision and then put the issue out of his mind, he sought in this instance for reassurance that the experts were recommending the right course. He had recently promoted a thoughtful young lawyer from his own home state of Missouri, Clark Clifford, to the post of White House counsel, and he asked Clifford to prepare for him a comprehensive survey of U.S.-Soviet relations. After talking with almost every knowledgeable person in the administration, Clifford delivered a report nearly a hundred thousand words in length. It confirmed everything that Truman had been told earlier. Describing the Soviet Union as bent on aggressive expansion, the report declared, "The language of military power is the only language which disciples of power politics understand." It therefore recommended a build-up in American military strength, accompanied by aid to "all democratic countries which are in any way menaced or endangered by the U.S.S.R." [44]

Fortified by this advice, Truman accepted in principle the recommendations of the experts. He evidenced doubt only as to whether Congress and the public would approve. Since support of the Iranian cause had seemed popular earlier in the year, he and his advisers decided that military supplies in limited quantities could be transferred directly to Iran. Pending a campaign to educate the public, they agreed, military assistance to Greece and Turkey should be channeled through the United Kingdom.[45]

This expedient proved unworkable. The ferocious European winter of 1946–47 laid bare the frailty of England's economy, and the British government gave formal warning that it could no longer carry chief responsibility for supporting the Greeks and Turks. Truman and the men around him saw themselves at a turning point. It was one thing to agree in private on an "inner conviction"; it was quite another to announce this conviction, to challenge the Soviet Union publicly, and test whether the American people would endorse a hazardous commitment in an unfamiliar and far-away region.

Given the consensus that had already developed, the administration's course of action was practically predetermined. Quick accord developed that the President should go before Congress and make a dramatic appeal for funds to aid Greece and Turkey. The only difference of opinion had to do with the scope and emphasis of the President's message—whether the message should confine itself to the Eastern Mediterranean or deal with global issues and whether stress should go to economic or to military aid requirements.

The President and his chief advisers conferred with congressional leaders. By this time, Byrnes had been replaced by General George Marshall, the war-time army chief of staff. A low-key presentation by Marshall, centering on the Eastern Mediterranean and the need for economic aid, evoked little response. Acheson, staying on temporarily as Marshall's Under Secretary, stepped in. As he recalls the occasion,

> No time was left for measured appraisal. In the past eighteen months, I said, Soviet pressure on the Straits, on Iran, and on northern Greece had brought the Balkans to a point where a highly possible Soviet break-through might open three continents ot Soviet penetration. Like apples in a barrel infected by one rotten one, the corrup-

tion of Greece would infect Iran and all to the east. It would also carry infection to Africa through Asia Minor and Egypt, and to Europe through Italy and France.

Arthur Vandenberg had become chairman of the Senate Foreign Relations Committee as a result of the Republican sweep the preceding November. He said that if the President spoke in such a fashion, Congress and the country would follow him.[46]

The eventual message was therefore both broad in character and militant in language. Stating what came to be called "the Truman Doctrine," the President declared, "It must be the policy of the United States to support free peoples who are resisting attempted subjugation by armed minorities or outside pressures." He explained,

> To ensure the peaceful development of nations, free from coercion, the United States has taken a leading part in establishing the United Nations. The United Nations is designed to make possible lasting freedom and independence for its members. We shall not realize our objectives, however, unless we are willing to help free peoples to maintain their free institutions and their national integrity against aggressive movements that seek to impose upon them totalitarian regimes. This is no more than a frank recognition that totalitarian regimes imposed on free peoples, by direct or indirect aggression, undermine the foundations of international peace and hence the security of the United States.

Although Truman said he believed the United States should provide primarily economic aid, he made it clear that he envisioned providing military supplies and U.S. military advisers.

In his message, Truman stated only briefly the argument that Acheson had made to the congressional leadership. He declared, "Should we fail to aid Greece and Turkey in this fateful hour, the effect will be far reaching to the West as well as the East." When open hearings were held on the proposed aid appropriations, however, Acheson served as chief witness, and he

harped on the string. Predicting that Soviet success in Turkey
would have repercussions in Iran, he went on to say,

> Iran borders on Afghanistan and India. . . . India
> carries us on to Burma and Indonesia, and Malaya, areas
> in French Indochina . . . and that carries you to China.
> . . . And what we are trying to point out is that a failure
> in these key countries would echo throughout that vast
> territory.[47]

Responding to such reasoning and to administration lobbying
on Capitol Hill and among the public, Congress voted aid to
Greece and Turkey 67 to 23 in the Senate and 287 to 107 in
the House.

The Truman Doctrine message, followed by its congressional
endorsement, did not mark the last stage in the commencement
of the Cold War. Not until after crises over Berlin, Czechoslovakia, and Italy in 1948 and the formation of NATO and the
communist success in China in 1949 did the relationship between the United States and the Soviet Union become one of
uncompromising antagonism. At present we lack documentary
evidence relating to those later developments. In any case, the
subsequent policy of the United States was to remain substantially that which developed during 1946 and found expression
in the President's proposal for aid to Greece and Turkey.

Of course, the administration might have made this choice
because Soviet actions in fact left the United States no reasonable option. Truman and Acheson say as much in their memoirs, and most interpretive writings of the 1950's and early
1960's take this to be the case. In retrospect, however, one can
see that the administration need not have perceived Soviet behavior exactly as it did.

In the first place, its members focused on some Soviet actions
and ignored others. In Finland, the Soviet authorities accepted
a non-communist regime subject to guarantees that it would
not be hostile. In Hungary, Soviet occupation commanders did
not interfere with elections, the results of which were a parlia-

ment overwhelmingly non-communist and a cabinet which had only one communist minister. They did not intervene to impose a communist regime until 1947—after the Truman Doctrine message. Up to that time, Hungary was no more a Soviet satellite than was Italy an Anglo-American satellite. In Czechoslovakia, similarly, the Russians tolerated a coalition government in which communists were not the dominant faction.

Yet Truman and his advisers apparently paid little attention to occurrences in Finland, Hungary, or Czechoslovakia. Instead, they took Soviet actions in Poland, Rumania, and Bulgaria to be indicative of what the Soviet government intended to do everywhere else.

In the second place, Truman and the men around him ascribed to Soviet machinations developments which might with equal plausibility have been explained in other ways. In hindsight, most of the available information concerning Yugoslavia shows clearly that Tito always acted with some degree of independence—perhaps not as much as, say, de Gaulle in France, but certainly more than Groza in Rumania or Dimitrov in Bulgaria. Yet until the Soviet-Yugoslav breach of 1948, Truman and his advisers took Tito to be simply a puppet of Moscow, and when the Yugoslavs threatened to seize Trieste, fired at overflying U.S. aircraft, or harassed American nationals, they blamed Stalin.

The leaders in the American government were aware that the Greek royal government was narrowly based and reactionary. Their offers of aid were accompanied by exhortations for reform. They were also aware of the historic rivalries between Greece and her Balkan neighbors. Yet they seemed to take it for granted that the Soviet Union instigated resistance to the Greek government and that arms and supplies flowed to the insurgents across the Yugoslav frontier at the instance of the Soviet and not the Yugoslav government. Similarly, they dismissed the possibility that the Azerbaijan issue might be partly the manufacture of Iranians rather than Russians.

The available evidence indicates that the perceptions of Truman and his advisers became less discriminating as time passed. When Tito first threatened to seize Trieste in April 1945 they entertained the hypothesis that he was acting on his own. When Truman and Byrnes first considered aid to Greece in November 1945 they acknowledged that the country might be near anarchy primarily for reasons internal to Greece, and they spoke of the external threat as coming from "its northern neighbors, which are none too friendly in any event." [48] By the end of 1946 they no longer saw anything in Eastern Europe, the Mediterranean, or the Middle East except a baleful Soviet Union.

Furthermore, their response to the presumed Soviet threat to Greece, Turkey, and Iran was not the only possible response or even the only one urged in their circle of advisers. Harriman, for example, was regarded by Truman and others as one of the best judges of Soviet affairs. Meeting with Forrestal and various navy officers in the autumn of 1946, he said that the Russians were not bent on war, at least in the near future, and that people in Washington underestimated the extent to which Moscow would bend in the face of strongly worded diplomatic notes. Although Kennan had led in trying to teach the politicians that the Soviet Union was not a friend and that it would take advantage of any opportunity to expand its power and influence, he, too, had emphasized firmness in diplomacy. He predicted, for example, that the Russians would not take any action in the Eastern Mediterranean or Middle East which might lead to a break in relations with Britain. When he saw a draft of the Truman Doctrine message, he protested that it was too universal, too uncompromising, and too war-like.[49] Truman and his counselors might have viewed the situations in Greece, Turkey, and Iran with less alarm and chosen another, less militant course of action.

If one concedes that the Truman administration had some leeway in how it perceived and reacted to events in the Eastern

Mediterranean and Middle East, the argument might be advanced that domestic considerations precluded the alternatives. Politicians were well aware that, even during the war, Roman Catholics had remained strongly anti-Soviet. Americans of Polish origin, most of whom were Catholics, had organized a ferocious campaign in 1944 against concessions to the Russians on Polish territorial or political issues. Knowing that the Democratic party depended on support from such groups, strategists for the Roosevelt administration had feared that the President's conciliatory attitude toward the Soviet Union might lose him votes and injure Democratic senatorial and congressional candidates. In that particular election year, such fears proved unfounded.[50]

The end of the war, the apparent Soviet intransigence over Poland, and the resurgence of communist parties in Soviet-occupied Germany, France, and Italy led to continued interest in foreign affairs and intensified feeling against the U.S.S.R. among these religious and ethnic groups. The same events, plus the uncovering of a Soviet spy ring in Canadian atomic energy laboratories, a minatory speech by Stalin in February 1946, and a speech at Fulton, Missouri, by former Prime Minister Churchill condemning the "iron curtain" in Eastern Europe, stimulated similar feeling among other segments of the public. Journalists and politicians predicted that the Republicans would win many votes by campaigning against the administration's "appeasement." In the winter of 1945–46 attacks along these lines were initiated by such Republican leaders as Governor Dwight Green of Illinois, Senator Homer Capehart of Indiana, House minority leader Joseph W. Martin of Massachusetts, and the two men who had symbolized bipartisan co-operation in building the United Nations, John Foster Dulles and Arthur Vandenberg. Meanwhile, polls reinforced the prediction. One in March 1946, for example, showed 71 per cent disapproving of Russian policy and 60 per cent judging the administration's approach to the Soviet Union "too soft." [51]

In February 1946, when Byrnes delivered a speech critical of the Russians, the response in newspapers and on Capitol Hill was overwhelmingly approving. When he supported the Iranian demand for Soviet withdrawal from Azerbaijan in the United Nations, the public reaction also seemed favorable.[52] Even so, congressional elections in the autumn saw the Republicans unseat almost one-fourth of the Democrats in the House and one-fifth of those in the Senate. Republicans won control of the two chambers for the first time since the Depression. And they made impressive gains in states such as New York, New Jersey, Pennsylvania, Ohio, Michigan, Wisconsin, and California, which had large numbers of Catholic voters. From these data, one might infer that the Truman administration adopted a militant posture toward the Soviet Union in hope of holding on to Catholic and ethnic voters, bettering its own standing in the polls, and improving Democratic prospects for 1948.

The records of deliberations within the administration show, however, that Truman and his advisers always doubted whether their decisions would command public support. Byrnes was surprised by the extent of approval for his action in the United Nations on the Azerbaijan question. When the secretaries and the chiefs of staff argued that the government should resolve to go to war if necessary over the Straits issue, they questioned only whether Congress and the public would understand the necessity for doing so. Until Truman, Marshall, and Acheson had their successful meeting with the congressional leadership, they remained uncertain whether aid to Greece and Turkey would carry the two houses. In all probability, the leaders in the administration, including the most experienced politicians among them, were continually amazed that Catholic and ethnic voters sustained an interest in foreign affairs, for members of these groups had seldom been conspicuous before 1939 among the public that kept close watch on international relations. Almost certainly, members of the administration persisted in assuming that the basic trends in

American opinion were toward pacifism and isolationism. It therefore seems unlikely that these men chose as they did because they calculated that doing so would yield gains in votes and poll showings. Rather, they discovered, somewhat to their surprise, that congressional and public opinion would not prevent their taking a stand that, for other reasons, they judged to be right.

A tidy explanation of the Truman administration's policy might be put together by combining this fact with those underlined earlier. It would run as follows: Truman and the advisers whom he selected were instinctively anti-communist and anti-Soviet. The State Department bureaucracy started out regarding the Soviet Union as a malign and hostile power. For their own reasons, the military quickly adopted the State Department view. The experts then campaigned to convert their superiors. Finding that militant opposition to the Soviets would not be politically costly and might even be profitable, the leaders of the government not only let themselves be converted but went all the way to declaring a Cold War.

Such an explanation, however, is inadequate. To accept it as complete would require an assumption that Truman and the men around him were prepared to hazard lives because of prejudice, gullibility, or cynical calculation of what might win votes. They were simply not of that stripe. Although Truman liked to be quick and decisive, he could not have elected to support Turkey "to the end" or to utter the "Truman Doctrine" without solemn certainty that he was making the wisest and best decision. Byrnes, Acheson, Forrestal, and others surrounding Truman shared with their chief a sense of grave responsibility. No explanation can suffice unless it tells us why able and strongly conscientious men saw the evidence which the bureaucracy arranged as revealing a danger to the American people of such magnitude as to justify the risk of war.

I see no alternative to the hypothesis that they saw such danger because, in the words of Acheson's biographer, the "im-

age of Hitler seared itself on the eyes of all who fought him." [53]
The men around Truman started out not only disliking the
communist philosophy and remembering with distaste the collectivization, the purges, and the opportunistic diplomacy of
the pre-war Soviet Union but also inwardly apprehensive that
a "totalitarian" Russia might behave toward other nations as
had the "totalitarian" Axis powers. This apprehension disclosed
itself not only in the analogizing that accompanied discussion
of control of nuclear weapons but also such musing as Forrestal's in January 1946, that it might be easy to ridicule analyses of the communist ideology but that "in the middle of that
laughter we always should remember that we also laughed
at Hitler." [54]

Poland, Rumania, and Bulgaria attracted notice while Finland, Czechoslovakia, and Hungary did not because the latent
question in the minds of American statesmen was whether
Stalin's Russia would expand as ruthlessly as had Japan, Italy,
and Germany. The evidence, especially as interpreted by Foreign Service observers, suggested an answer in the affirmative.
The parallel seemed all the stronger because of the role of native communists in East European countries, for all Americans
had been taught (erroneously, as we now know) that indige-
nous "fifth columns" aided Fascist and Nazi conquests. However, neither Truman nor any of his high-level advisers drew a
firm conclusion from these cases.

When reports then came in concerning Azerbaijan, Russian
pressure on Turkey, and outside aid to the Greek insurgents,
American leaders felt themselves driven to the verdict which
they had earlier resisted. They saw a China incident succeed-
ing a Manchurian incident, a Spanish Civil War following
upon an Italo-Ethiopian War, a Czechoslovakian crisis suc-
ceeding an Anschluss. Convinced that "appeasement" of "totalitarian" states in the 1930's had merely encouraged aggression, Truman and his advisers felt impelled to resist the
"totalitarian" Soviet Union now, before its appetite fed upon

itself, Soviet power increased, and the people of the United States and other countries faced a Moloch more horrible than those to which so many lives had so recently been sacrificed.

The evidence that American official thinking was dominated by a single historical parallel is not so clear as it is for postwar planning during World War II. And it is even harder to express a judgment that, if this was the case, the results deserve criticism. The "revisionist" view of the Soviet government as preoccupied with its own recovery and security rests on no better evidence than the traditional view that Stalin aimed at conquering for communism as much territory as he could seize without involving his nation in a new world war. In any case, there is no way of disproving the hypothesis that, if forces friendly to the Soviet Union had gained control in Greece and Iran, the consequence would have been to encourage Soviet expansionism, produce an outward drive such as Truman and his advisers supposed already to exist, and end in a confrontation which the United States could not elude. Moreover, one has to recognize that, however dreadful the Cold War may have been, it was better than a genuine war; and a genuine war did not occur.

As in the preceding chapter, I am not criticizing what the American government did, but merely pointing out that members of the Truman administration appear to have thought about the issues before them in a frame of reference made up in part of historical analogies, parallels, and presumed trends and that the history employed for this purpose was narrowly selected and subjected to no deliberate scrutiny or analysis.

III

Korea, 1950:
History Overpowering Calculation

The strength with which parallels of the 1930's gripped the minds of Truman and his associates was demonstrated in the administration's decision to intervene in Korea in 1950. Whether it was equally influential in other major decisions of the period 1947–50, we cannot now judge. At the moment when I write, records of internal administration debate in those relatively long-ago years remain classified. Hence they are closed to scholars outside the government. Information concerning the Korean decision is available only because a full-scale congressional inquiry in 1951 exposed issues which members of the administration felt obliged to address in memoirs and which journalists and scholars followed up by means of interviews.

In this one, amply documented case, the evidence indicates that the administration had evolved a deliberate policy of avoiding any military engagement in the Korean peninsula. It then reversed itself in a moment of crisis, and it did so primarily because the President and his advisers perceived a North Korean attack on South Korea as analogous to instances of Japanese, Italian, and German aggression prior to World War II.

At the end of that war, Americans had found themselves occupying southern Korea. They had not planned to do so. At Cairo in 1943 Roosevelt promised Korea independence "in due course." So far as White House records reveal, he spent no thought on how this pledge might be carried out. At Yalta, he suggested an international trusteeship. It would last only until the Koreans organized their own government and involve no occupation by foreign troops. Aware of Tsarist interest in the peninsula, Roosevelt probably had in mind assuring Stalin of post-war influence without actual Soviet control. Apparently, he had as yet no notion how trusteeship might work in practice.[1]

As late as the Potsdam conference of July 1945 the American government had no plan for putting forces into Korea.[2] Then came the unexpected Japanese surrender. Since the Red Army had just begun to move, Korea remained wholly in Japanese hands. Seeing a possible counter for later bargaining with Moscow, people in the State Department pressed for a dash to occupy some of the country. The new Secretary of State, James F. Byrnes, liked the idea and overrode resistance from the army. An all-night conference at the Pentagon produced a directive that General MacArthur take possession up to the thirty-eighth parallel, just north of Seoul. (Two staff officers concluded that this was the best line that could be attained; one was Colonel Dean Rusk.)[3]

With the Soviets offering no protest, two American divisions sailed north from Okinawa and took control of southern Korea. General John R. Hodge served as commander and military governor. A bluff combat soldier, he entered a situation that would have bewildered an officer of much more subtle intelligence. He found most Koreans believing the Cairo declaration had promised immediate independence, for their language had no character for "in due course." Hundreds of politicians and political organizations offered to form governments. Equipped neither by the army nor the State Department with aides who knew anything about Korea, Hodge made haphazard choices among these volunteers. Meanwhile, he met with no co-operation whatever from the Russians north of the thirty-eighth parallel toward fulfillment of the goal set for him by the War Department—establishment of a unified administration for Korea and prompt withdrawal of the occupying forces.[4]

Whether rightly or wrongly, Hodge began to suspect the Koreans with whom he had become associated of being communists. Aware that the Russians were backing communist groups in the north, he became fearful of finding himself administering a communist country. With some misgivings, Hodge therefore started supporting right-wing Koreans. His consistent objective, however, was merely to create a Korean administration to which he could safely turn over his responsibilities. From the first, his aim was to get American forces out of the country at the earliest possible moment.[5]

Officials in the State Department had a different outlook. There, Korea concerned the Assistant Secretary for Occupied Areas and the Office of Far Eastern Affairs. The former had greater understanding of and sympathy for Hodge's point of view, for the Assistant Secretary was John H. Hilldring, a lean, bull-throated general who had earlier managed occupation planning for the Joint Chiefs. But even Hilldring felt hesitancy about early evacuation of Korea. Responsible for begging occupation costs from Congress, he had to assure conservative appropriations committees that spending on Korea did not simply build up an eventual Soviet satellite. Fearing that this would be the outcome if American troops pulled out, he argued for prolonging their stay.[6]

The Office of Far Eastern Affairs argued against withdrawal more vigorously. Its successive chiefs, John Carter Vincent and W. Walton Butterworth, were preoccupied with China and, to a lesser extent, Japan. In China they hoped for some compromise between Chiang Kai-shek and the communists, creating a unified, peaceful, independent, and friendly Chinese nation. To this end, they wanted Soviet help in bringing the Chinese communists to terms. In regard to Japan, they wanted Soviet acquiescence in arrangements giving MacArthur sole say in the military government and, ultimately, Soviet agreement to a Japanese peace treaty. While most of them knew and cared little about Korea, they saw American withdrawal as something the Soviets would want and hence a negotiating chip.[7]

Higher officials in the State Department shared this view. Since war-time records suggested that Stalin was less interested in Asia than in Europe and since discussion of Asian questions could be bilateral, involving neither the British nor the French, Secretary Byrnes opened the Moscow foreign ministers conference of December 1945 with proposals on the Far East. He hoped agreement on these might set a precedent for accords on more difficult issues elsewhere. He asked of the Russians that they support American mediation efforts in China and acknowledge MacArthur's authority in Japan. In return, he offered the establishment of a commission to advise MacArthur, on which the Soviets would be represented, and he proposed that a joint American-Soviet commission arrange a provisional government for all of Korea and lay plans to make Korea completely independent within five years. With some changes in language, the Russians accepted Byrnes's terms. Chiefly for this reason, Byrnes went home deeming the Moscow conference a success.[8]

Optimism in Washington proved short-lived. The Soviet experts warned that the Russians would settle for nothing less than a communist Korea, and the behavior of Soviet members of the joint commission seemed to bear out this prophecy. The Moscow agreement had called for consultation with all "democratic" elements. As in Eastern Europe, the Russians interpreted "democratic" as applying solely to communists and their allies. By May 1946 it seemed clear that no co-operation would materialize. Ruefully, Byrnes agreed that the American command should move to organize a provisional government simply within its own zone.[9]

While the Far Eastern specialists in the department endorsed such a step, they continued to oppose early withdrawal of the American occupation force. Though well aware of Hodge's and the army's undiminished eagerness to get out, they held it of great importance that Korea neither be allowed to fall to the communists unrequited nor be relinquished to right-wing elements likely to provoke a civil war.

By some means not discoverable in available records, the State Department won the President's support. It happened that Edwin W. Pauley, a California oil magnate serving as White House adviser on reparations, paid a brief visit to Korea in June 1946. Upon his return, he wrote Truman a letter, declaring that Korea deserved more attention and recommending a large-scale aid program. The task of drafting a reply fell to Vincent. He drew up a letter endorsing in emphatic terms the position which his office had been defending within the government. The President signed it.

In this letter, Truman expressed complete agreement with Pauley's description of Korea as "an ideological battleground upon which our entire success in Asia may depend." He continued,

> Korea has been for many decades the focus of international rivalries and I consider one of the principal objectives of our policy there to be to prevent Korea from again becoming the source of future conflict. . . . I believe that the most effective way to meet the situation in Korea is to intensify and persevere in our present efforts to build up a self-governing and democratic Korea, neither subservient to nor menacing any power. . . .
>
> Our commitments for the establishment of an inde-

pendent Korea require that we stay in Korea long enough
to see the job through and that we have adequate personnel and sufficient funds to do a good job.[10]

This letter was followed by one to the secretaries of War and
the Navy, also drafted in Vincent's office, offering support for
proposals to spend additional sums on aid to Korea. It said,
"I am convinced that we may be required to stay in Korea
a considerable length of time." [11]

Truman certainly did not sign such communications off-
hand. Especially since they involved money, he must have
discussed them not only with State Department representatives
but also with one or more members of the Budget Bureau
and his own staff. Nevertheless, it is more than plausible that
the arguments to which he attended had little to do with
Korea. A display of firmness in the Far East, he was probably
told, would strengthen the hand of General Marshall, then
on a special diplomatic assignment mediating in China. It
would be a partial reply to those in Congress and elsewhere
who criticized efforts for accommodation with the Chinese
communists. The administration had just weathered a battle
in behalf of a substantial loan to Britain, and a proposal to
aid Korea would counteract the charge of concern for Europe
at the expense of Asia. If the money were spent on American-
produced goods, there could be benefit to the domestic economy. Since neither Hodge nor the army had yet elaborated a
case for early troop withdrawal, counter-arguments were few.
The President probably judged the case so clear as to call
for little reflection.

The State Department victory turned out, however, to be
only temporary. Still occupied primarily with China, the Far
Eastern specialists took their time in developing an actual aid
program. It was February 1947 before they settled on a proposal that six hundred million dollars in goods and money be
devoted to Korean aid in fiscal 1948, 1949, and 1950. By that
time, the Marshall mission had come to an end, with General

Marshall advising the President not to hope for peace in China. Crises with the Soviet Union had developed in Turkey and Iran, and the administration had decided to take over support for the Turks and Greeks from the British. Thought in Washington about economic aid turned to those projects that soon took form in the Marshall Plan. Large-scale aid to Korea became distinctly second-order business.[12] Of what the State Department had won in the summer of 1946, there remained chiefly the President's written pledge that the United States would stick it out in the peninsula.

The army viewed this pledge as unwise. In April 1947 Secretary of War Robert Patterson cautioned Marshall, now Secretary of State, that the American zone in Korea could dissolve into anarchy at any moment. If so, American forces would have to scramble out. "I am convinced," wrote Patterson, "that the United States should pursue forcefully a course of action whereby we get out of Korea at an early date." [13] Military officers emphasized that Korea had no strategic value to the United States. In response to an inquiry from Marshall, the Joint Chiefs explained that they would expect to bypass the peninsula if conducting operations in Siberia or China and that air attack alone could neutralize its usefulness to an enemy.[14]

Even within the State Department, the Far Eastern specialists found support dwindling. Joseph E. Jacobs, a senior Foreign Service officer sent out to advise Hodge, sent back increasingly pessimistic reports. He cabled in July that "events are forcing us into a position where we may be compelled for reasons of expediency (opposition to the Soviets) to support extreme rightist leaders such as [Syngman] Rhee." If South Korea were judged militarily important, Jacobs advised in September, then a much more strenuous effort should be made to build a South Korean nation. If it were not so judged, he said, the United States should "get out as quickly and gracefully as possible." George Kennan, now heading the department's Policy Planning Staff, seconded this recommendation. According to one official, there was "fairly unanimous agreement to abandon the Koreans to their fate," the grounds being "that Southern Korea is without strategic value to us, is, in fact, a strategic liability, and . . . that there are likewise no political reasons (in the short-term sense) which impel us to remain in Korea." [15]

The Soviet government meanwhile proposed that all foreign troops be promptly removed from Korea. With the Far Eastern specialists arguing that the result would inevitably be a Soviet or North Korean take-over of the whole peninsula, Secretary Marshall decided to counter with a proposal for United Nations-supervised elections in both occupation zones. The General Assembly adopted this resolution. Although the Soviet occupation authorities refused to co-operate, the American command won approval from Washington for holding elections only in the American zone. As a result, a provisional government for the Republic of Korea came into being, with Syngman Rhee as its chief.

The decision to proceed with elections implied a decision to end the American military occupation. The President reviewed the specific question in the forum of the newly established National Security Council. There, the secretaries of State and Defense, the service secretaries, and assorted others had opportunity to discuss a written recommendation from the Joint Chiefs advocating withdrawal. With the President in the chair, the Council gave its formal approval. Although the full text of the document is not yet accessible, it appears to have provided that the United States would pull its forces out at the point at which the new Korean regime developed a defense force capable of maintaining internal security. Once this force existed, the United States was to leave Korea to its fate. One sentence in the NSC paper read: "The United States should not become so irrevocably involved in the Korean situation that an action taken by any faction in Korea or by any other power in Korea could be considered a 'casus belli' for the United States." [16]

The NSC paper of April 1948 projected American troop withdrawal by the end of the year. The Far Eastern specialists in State nevertheless continued to work for keeping the forces there. Because of the worsening situation in China, they had come under attack in Congress and the press, and their ranks were thinning. Even so, they mounted an effective delaying campaign. When the Soviets announced in September 1948 that they would remove their occupation forces by December, the American government did not follow suit. As an army historian summarizes the reasoning, "the Russian eagerness to have all foreign troops leave the peninsula cast doubts upon the sagacity of the U.S. withdrawal program. The possibility of the Communists using force to unify the country while the ROK Government was weak and conditions were unsettled argued against a quick evacuation of South Korea." In October the South Korean police and army just barely succeeded in suppressing a series of large-scale local uprisings. Although these events might have been taken as warning of precisely the type of trouble envisioned in the NSC paper, the State Department specialists argued, according to the same army historian, "Since ROK defense forces were not properly prepared to resist invasion . . . the continued presence of U.S. forces would have a stabilizing effect upon the over-all situation." [17] And 1948 came to a close with most of Hodge's force still in place.

Discussion of the April NSC paper had apparently skirted the question of whether American troops should be withdrawn and kept out, even if the result were North Korean conquest of the South. Indeed, the President had given his approval on assurance that South Korea's "prospects for survival may be considered favorable as long as it can continue to receive large-scale aid from the U.S." [18] In effect, State Department officials insisted that the question be confronted.

In December 1948 the United Nations General Assembly voted in favor of withdrawal of all occupation forces from Korea. Since the United States could still sway a majority of votes in the organization, this resolution could not have passed if the Far Eastern specialists had induced Secretary Marshall to try to defeat it. If they tried to do so, they failed; and the result was to cast the issue in terms of whether or not to comply with a directive from the United Nations.

The army prepared for renewed debate by once again consulting the commanders in the Far East. General MacArthur responded with a flat assertion that his occupation command in Japan could not train and equip a South Korean army capable of withstanding a North Korean invasion. He said further, "It should be recognized that in the event of any serious threat to the security of Korea, strategic and military considerations will force abandonment of any pretense of military support." MacArthur recommended withdrawal of Hodge's forces by May 1949. When Secretary of the Army Kenneth Royall called on him in Tokyo, MacArthur reiterated this recommendation, and Royall reported it to the President.[19]

In March the National Security Council once again devoted a session to Korea. Now having MacArthur's statements to reinforce the arguments in earlier memoranda, the Council reaffirmed its 1948 decision. State Department opponents of withdrawal won, as their only solace, agreement that withdrawal be completed in June instead of May and that a 500-man military advisory group remain behind.[20]

At almost the last moment, the army chief of staff, General Omar Bradley, evidenced misgivings. Rhee had asked publicly what the United States would do in the event of a North Korean invasion. Although the new civilian head of the American mission in Seoul, John J. Muccio, put him off by replying that the improved military strength of South Korea made such a contingency unlikely, Rhee retorted, "What we are trying to find out is whether or not the United States considers that Southern Korea falls within its own first line of defense." Perhaps prompted by Rhee's persistent questioning, Bradley circulated among his fellow chiefs a memorandum entitled "Implications of a Possible Full-Scale Invasion from North Korea Subsequent to Withdrawal of U.S. Troops from Korea." As one of his army colleagues summarizes Bradley's memorandum: "He recommended that in such event United States nationals be evacuated and the aggression be reported to the U.N. Security Council as a threat to international peace. Depending on the action of the United Nations Security Council, a composite United Nations force might be introduced to check the aggression." In such event, Bradley implied, some American forces might go back into Korea.[21]

The other chiefs of staff, however, overruled Bradley. Reemphasizing the opinion delivered in 1947, they agreed on the following dicta:

> From the strategic viewpoint, the position of the Joint Chiefs of Staff regarding Korea, summarized briefly, is that Korea is of little strategic value to the United States and that any commitment to United States use of military force in Korea would be ill-advised and impracticable in view of the potentialities of the over-all world situation and of our heavy international obligations as compared with our current military strength.[22]

The withdrawal of American occupation forces from Korea was completed at the end of June.

With the triumph of Mao over Chiang and cries in Congress for the heads of the men who had "lost China," the Far Eastern specialists in the State Department lost whatever strength they had once possessed. When Truman made over his cabinet after being inaugurated in his own right in January 1949, he allowed Marshall to retire and called Dean Acheson back to be Secretary of State. Reorganizing the department, Acheson created independent assistant secretaryships for each of the geographical regions. Although he showed moral support for Butterworth by naming him the first Assistant Secretary for Far Eastern Affairs, he soon replaced him with Dean Rusk, who, after leaving the army to join the State Department, had been concerned primarily with United Nations affairs and had as yet made few enemies in Congress. For advice regarding Korea, Acheson looked chiefly to Rusk, Ambassador-at-Large Philip C. Jessup, and others previously little involved with Asian affairs.[23] Although we do not yet know what these counselors told Acheson, we do know that Jessup passed along at least one memorandum (prepared by Professor Owen Lattimore of Johns Hopkins) which recommended that the United States "disembarrass itself as quickly as possible of entanglements in South Korea." We also know that when Jessup visited Seoul early in 1950 he told members of the national assembly in emphatic terms that Korea would have to make its own way in the world without excessive dependence on American help.[24] It seems probable that the men who now had the ear of the Secretary of State regarded the position embodied in the National Security Council papers of 1948 and 1949, which had the President's approval, as the position of the United States. Certainly, State Department sources entered no demurrer to newspaper and magazine stories saying that, with American troops out, the United States no longer had any responsibility for defending South Korea against an attack from the north.[25]

The firmness of this position should not be exaggerated. Except in intra-mural consideration of the Bradley memorandum by the Joint Chiefs, the contingency of a North Korean attack on the South appears to have received little attention. Secretary Acheson testified later that, while surveys of possible crisis areas touched on Korea, it was never a favorite. "The view was generally held," he recalled, "that since the Communists had far from exhausted the potentialities for obtaining their objectives through guerrilla and psychological warfare, political pressure and stimulation, such means would probably continue to be used rather than overt military aggression." [26] Although Americans in Seoul sometimes warned of weaknesses in the Korean government and army, people in Washington apparently attended only to signals suggesting that they had no cause for worry. To his subsequent embarrassment, the chief administrator of American foreign-aid programs assured a Senate committee in early June 1950 that South Korea had a "well-disciplined army of 100,000 soldiers; one that is prepared to meet any challenge by North Korean forces." [27]

Insofar as civilians in the Truman administration showed concern, it was lest South Korea attack the North. Rhee's hostility to the Russians and to the communists in Pyongyang had been manifest from the outset. When the Department of the Army first authorized the equipping of a South Korean defense force, its directives emphasized the need to prevent that force from acting "in an aggressive manner." Royall apparently found renewed reason to fear a move north, and officials preparing fiscal 1950 and 1951 aid packages for Korea carefully limited military supplies to light vehicles and weapons.[28] Acheson's celebrated National Press Club speech of January 1950 warning that the United States could not undertake to defend positions outside a defensive perimeter bounded by Japan, the Ryukyus, and the Philippines may have been phrased in part to dissuade Rhee from counting on American forces to rescue him if he acted and got into trouble.[29]

Insofar as American officials reflected at all upon the possibility of North Korean aggression, they apparently took it as a foregone conclusion that the United States should not and would not resist with force. Acheson's Press Club speech set forth a reasonably well-developed political rationale for the position that the Joint Chiefs had advocated on the basis of military logic.

At the time, much more attention was going to Taiwan than to Korea. Chiang's remnants had taken refuge there; the victorious communists were expected to attack them; and Chiang's partisans in Congress and the newspaper and magazine worlds demanded that the American government defend the island. Applying much the same reasoning as in the case of Korea, the Joint Chiefs advised "that overt United States military action to deny Communist domination of Formosa would not be justified." [30] On January 5, 1950, the President announced that the American government would not interfere, even to the extent of providing Chiang with military aid and advice. This statement caused outcries, and Acheson's speech of a week later had the aim of justifying the entire stance of the United States in the Pacific and East Asia.

In the speech Acheson argued that the future of Asia would be determined by Asians. To the extent that the Soviet Union sought to impose its doctrine or system on China and Chinese borderlands, he predicted, it would arouse "the righteous anger, and the wrath, and the hatred of the Chinese people." If the American government intervened to counter the Soviets, it would draw some of this wrath. Americans might offer to share their wealth, knowledge, and experience, recognizing, however, that their aid would never have more than marginal effects. Otherwise, their posture should be to refrain from interfering in the processes of self-determination and self-development. Logically, it followed that the United States should avoid warfare unless driven to action by an assault on its own defense perimeter.

After describing that perimeter as embracing neither Taiwan nor Korea nor any other part of mainland Asia, Acheson went on to assert, "So far as the military security of other areas of the Pacific is concerned, it must be clear that no person can guarantee these areas against military attack." He added as a qualifier that "Should . . . an attack occur . . . the initial reliance must be on the people attacked to resist it and then upon the commitments of the entire civilized world under the Charter of the United Nations which so far has not proved a weak reed to lean on by any people who are determined to protect their independence against outside aggression."

When accused later of having invited an invasion of South Korea, Acheson defended himself by quoting this latter passage. It seems probable, however, that his Press Club speech embodied an assumption that the United States would not and should not go to war for the sake of preventing South Korea's fall.

The Press Club speech was followed, to be sure, by efforts to obtain appropriations for aid to Korea, and these efforts necessarily entailed assurances to Congress that South Korea was important to the United States. As it happened, the administration paid relatively little attention to the Korean aid bill when it lay before the House of Representatives. A combination formed in opposition. It consisted of opponents of all aid, supporters of Chiang critical of the administration's handling of Chinese and Taiwanese affairs, extreme conservatives who regarded the Rhee regime as socialist, and a few men on the left who viewed Rhee as a dictator. Together they formed a temporary majority and defeated the bill, 193 to 191. To rescue the measure, the President and Secretary of State published statements describing failure to assist South Korea as potentially "disastrous." The chief of the Economic Cooperation Administration felt impelled to testify that "we are stemming communism," and the director of the Korean program that "it is in the national interest of the United States to keep 20,000,000 people from going into the Communist orbit." The bill was retrieved and carried through both houses.[31]

That administration leaders spoke less categorically in private conversation with members of Congress is, however, suggested by an extemporaneous comment made in May 1950 by chairman Connally of the Senate Foreign Relations Committee. Asked whether abandonment of Korea was under consideration, he replied,

> I'm afraid it's going to be seriously considered because I'm afraid it's going to happen, whether we want it to or not. . . . South Korea is cut right across by this line—north of it are the Communists with access to the mainland—and Russia is over there on the mainland. So that whenever she takes a notion she can overrun Korea just like she will probably overrun Formosa when she gets ready to do it.[32]

It was the policy of the United States in June 1950 to avoid using American military forces in Korea. This had been the consistent position of the Joint Chiefs, twice considered by the National Security Council, and on both occasions approved by the President. In the Press Club speech, the Secretary of State made a declaration to this effect, and the chairman of the key Senate committee did likewise. Though with some of the sloppiness inevitable in any complex organization, the government can be said to have coolly assessed the national interest and decided what decision ought to be made in the event of a seemingly improbable contingency.

On Saturday, June 24, 1950, the contingency materialized. The actual decisions proved to be the opposite of those calculated in advance.[33]

Reliable reports of the invasion arrived around nine p.m. The State Department duty officer summoned Assistant Secretary Rusk from a dinner party at columnist Joseph Alsop's house. Accompanied by fellow guest Secretary of the Army Frank Pace, Rusk hurried to the department. He called in John D. Hickerson, the Assistant Secretary for United Nations Affairs. After conferring with Hickerson, Rusk telephoned Acheson. By the time of Acheson's arrival, Rusk and Hickerson were ready to recommend an appeal to the United Nations Security Council. Acheson approved, telephoned the President in Independence, Missouri, and before 11:30 that night, procured Truman's consent. With the Soviet representative absent and thus unable to impose a veto, the U.S. ambassador to the United Nations obtained on the following day a Security Council resolution calling on North Korea to cease hostilities and withdraw.

Meanwhile, officials in State and Defense tried to sort out what was happening in Korea. Acheson kept in touch with Truman by telephone. Early on Sunday afternoon, Truman decided to fly back to Washington. That evening, he met with Acheson, Under Secretary of State James Webb, Hickerson, Rusk, Ambassador-at-Large Jessup, Secretary of Defense Louis Johnson, the three service secretaries, Joint Chiefs chairman Omar Bradley, and the chiefs of staff of the army, navy, and the air force. Because of repair work in the central part of the White House, Truman held the session across the street at Blair House, ordinarily a residence for official guests. Discussion went on for about three hours, concluding with a presidential decision to step up transfer of military equipment to South Korea.

Monday, June 26, brought reports not only that North Korea would, as expected, disregard the United Nations appeal but also that the North Korean army was punching through South Korea's lines like a swordsman attacking a stretched canvas. That night, Truman met again at Blair House with Acheson, Rusk, Hickerson, Jessup, Johnson, Pace, air force secretary Thomas K. Finletter, Bradley, and the chiefs of staff of the army and air force. At the end of an hour's talk, the President authorized American air and naval action in support of South Korea.

Despite air force and carrier air attacks on North Korean tank and infantry columns, pins marking their locations steadily moved southward on Washington battle maps. On the afternoon of Thursday, June 29, the President agreed to military recommendations that bombing be authorized north of the thirty-eighth parallel and that a small army contingent be landed to keep open the southeast Korean post of Pusan. Meanwhile, with Truman's approval, MacArthur made a hazardous personal reconnaissance of the front.

By Friday morning, Truman had before him MacArthur's recommendation that a regimental combat team be landed at Pusan and that two American divisions in Japan be readied for prompt commitment to battle. In a five a.m. telephone conversation with the Secretary of the Army, Truman approved dispatch of the first regiment. A few hours later, he met at the White House with Acheson, Johnson, Deputy Secretary of Defense Stephen Early, and the chiefs of staff. He also invited Averell Harriman, now an ambassador-at-large, who had on his own initiative flown in from Paris. In a matter of half an hour, Truman there decided to follow MacArthur's advice. Indeed, he authorized the commitment of all available forces and promised to call up reserves and otherwise mobilize to ensure that South Korea not be conquered. Following a line of action quite contrary to that foreshadowed in three previous years of planning, the President elected to treat defense of South Korea as a national interest justifying expenditure of life and large sums of money and some risk of precipitating general war.

Why did he do so?

Inspecting the sequence of events just sketched, one might assume that Truman actually made a series of incremental decisions: first, to ask for a United Nations resolution; second, to provide military supplies to Rhee's forces; third, to commit American air and naval units; fourth, to send a regiment to Pusan; and, only at the last, to engage to defend South Korea no matter what the cost. Participants so perceived the successive telephone conferences and meetings at Blair House and the White House. Truman himself did so. When informing congressional leaders that the air force and navy would act, he minimized the likelihood of employing ground troops. When the possibility of sending in the army came up at a special Thursday afternoon meeting of the National Security Council, some members sensed that the President was troubled and hesitant.[34] After approving dispatch of regiment to Pusan, Truman still withheld for hours a final decision to send in division-size forces. Plainly, he assumed that he retained some discretion down to the final moment.

In retrospect, however, it seems plain that the President made his basic choice during the first twenty-four hours. Before leaving Independence, Truman instructed Acheson to bring the chiefs of staff to that evening's meeting at Blair House.[35] This fact may not have significance, for Truman would probably have wanted the visible blessing of the military, regardless of what he chose to do. Possibly, however, American military action already figured in his thoughts.

At the Kansas City airport, Truman told reporters, "It could be a dangerous situation. I hope it isn't." A member of his staff said to one newspaperman, however, "The boss is going to hit those fellows hard." After arriving in Washington, Truman himself used the phrase. In the limousine carrying him from National Airport to the White House, he told Louis Johnson that he intended to "hit them hard." [36]

At the Blair House meeting that evening, Truman gave out similar signals. Over a pre-dinner drink, he said to Acheson, "We can't let the U.N. down." Although he initiated general conversation after attendants had cleared away the dessert dishes by asserting that he had a completely "open mind," almost everyone present could sense his inclination. The questions which he pressed had to do with the readiness of American forces in Asia, the ability of the air force and navy to check the North Koreans unaided by ground troops, and the time needed to shift the American divisions in Japan to Korea. Summing up the meeting, Jessup recalled the "hard core of resolve" displayed and the evident willingness to accept the risk of a new world war.[37]

On Monday morning, long before Acheson recommended

air and naval support for South Korea, Truman talked with Senator Connally, indicating that he contemplated committing American forces without asking consent from Congress. Connally encouraged him to do so, observing, "You might run into a long debate . . . which would tie your hands completely." On the same morning, Truman pointed to Korea on a globe and commented to a member of his staff, "This is the Greece of the Far East. If we are tough enough now there won't be any next step." Receiving the South Korean ambassador that afternoon and being told that Rhee and his commanders were near despair, Truman cited as a comforting analogy the plight of Britain and France in 1917, prior to American intervention. When he subsequently authorized air and naval action, he did not speak of his commitment as limited. Everything he had done in the previous five years, he said, had "been to try to avoid making a decision such as I made tonight." [38] Although four days elapsed before his final order for all-out ground warfare, his advisers assumed that, if the military recommended such action, the President would order it. Even the commanders in the field made such an assumption.

Truman, of course, took one action at a time. He waited on events. Until certain that the South Koreans could not check the invasion by themselves, he withheld any American military commitment. Until advised that air force and navy support would not be enough, he withheld sending in the army. Throughout the week, he asked repeatedly whether there were signs that violence might break out elsewhere. Though never doubting that the Soviets had planned the North Korean action, he remained perplexed as to why they had chosen that particular move. Apprehensive lest it turn out to be a gambit, drawing American forces to a non-vital sector so as to open a breach somewhere else, Truman felt that he should stay his hand as long as possible. Barring either a favorable turn in Korea itself or a crisis elsewhere, however, he determined to treat defense of Korea as a vital interest, and he executed this reversal during the first day after the invasion.

Given that Truman's mind seemed set at least by the time he left Independence for Washington, one might adopt the view that, in reality, he had no choice to make. Although his own account emphasizes the complexity and difficulty of the decision-making process, he portrays his actions as almost inevitable. Indeed, hindsight commentary by all officials suggests that the decision to intervene in force was one which would have been made in the same circumstances by any reasonable man of ordinary prudence.[39]

In truth, the President probably had a wider range of choice than either he or his associates perceived in retrospect. Even the initial decision to ask for Security Council action need not have gone as it did. Dean Rusk chanced to be the key Assistant Secretary of State. Previously assigned to international organization affairs, he had a nearly fanatical belief in the long-run importance of the Charter and the United Nations, and it was Rusk who brought into the inner circle that first night the Assistant Secretary for United Nations Affairs. In a group so composed, the weight of opinion naturally went in one direction.

Had Under Secretary Webb or George Kennan been present, the balance might have tipped otherwise. Since Kennan was number three man in the department, the duty officer actually tried to reach him, but he was resting over the weekend in a farmhouse without a telephone. When able to comment later, he expressed some surprise at the U.N.'s taking "cognizance of what was, in the formal sense, a civil war." [40]

No necessity compelled the American government to propose Security Council action. No longer an occupying power, the United States had no special responsibility for Korea. Given other advice or a greater disposition toward caution, the Secretary of State and the President might have chosen at the outset to let the North Korean invasion come before the world organization at the instance of the United Nations observation team stationed on the thirty-eighth parallel. They could have taken the posture that the United States would be concerned as a signer of the Charter and a member of the Security Council but not necessarily more concerned than any other state so situated. As it was, neither man questioned a recommendation which had the effect of making the North Korean aggression not only a test of the United Nations but, in the first instance, a test of American influence in and commitment to the United Nations.

Even after the American delegate obtained a resolution from the Security Council, the President still need not have opted for American military action. The small military advisory group in Seoul had a well-developed plan for evacuating its own personnel and other Americans in Korea. Indeed, consistent with what was understood to be American policy, this was the only operation plan for Korea filed in any American headquarters.[41] Truman could have adopted the position that if North Korea refused to heed the Security Council appeal, the appropriate United Nations action was a vote of censure, followed perhaps by the application of economic sanctions. The President could have held that these measures should precede consideration of a naval blockade or punishment of the people of North Korea by aerial bombardment or other military measures. It was by no means self-evident that prompt military action would be less costly than well-prepared action later, even if United Nations forces started with no beachhead remaining in Korea. In fact, it is not apparent now that the amphibious landing at Inchon in September could not have been carried out just as successfully then or later if the North Koreans had meanwhile taken over all of South Korea. Truman could have elected to be deliberate and to exhaust other resources before turning to violence. He chose otherwise.

Most of the foregoing implies that the question to be answered is why the President chose as he did. One might argue that the decision or decisions were those of the government, with the President merely running to stay in the lead. And it is surely true that, from the first stage onward, Truman received little or no advice in favor of treating the North Korean attack as more a problem for the United Nations than the United States or for considering military action as a last recourse.

On balance, however, the evidence indicates not that the President was led but that he did lead. When telephoning reports from Washington to Independence, Acheson apparently urged nothing more than that the case be taken to the United Nations. While Louis Johnson disclosed to Truman in the limousine from National Airport that his own preference was for prompt and tough reaction, he did so only after hearing Truman speak of hitting them hard. At the first Blair House meeting, it was the President, not his advisers, who gave the cue for discussion of American military operations. In fact, Bradley said that the Joint Chiefs had not changed their opinion about Korea, and more than one of the conferees spoke against committing ground troops. At the second such conference Bradley and others from the military establishment emphasized the difficulty of fighting in Korea. It was Truman's choice to refrain from inviting arguments that might put in doubt the basic resolve to which he had so promptly come.

On the morning after the second Blair House meeting, the best-informed reporters in Washington described the majority of officials as deeming Korea of little value and military operations there as too costly to justify armed intervention.[42] For the most part, Democrats in Congress expressed willingness to accept the President's decisions, whatever they were. While some Republicans spoke of the North Korean action as yet another result of Roosevelt's and Truman's mismanagement of foreign affairs, the Senate Republican Policy Committee formally resolved that the United States had a "moral commitment" to South Korea but no obligation to go to war in its behalf.[43] Had the President inclined toward a different course, the bureaucracy and the country would apparently have followed him.

To explain or analyze American intervention in Korea, one must therefore focus on President Truman. Why did he react as he did? Why did he put out of his mind almost all that he had heard earlier about the strategic insignificance of the peninsula and its disadvantages as a battle area? Why did he display an almost automatic preference for a militant course of action?

Part of the answer doubtless lies in Truman's style, temperament, and mental make-up. His personality had developed in a migratory childhood in rural Missouri. After service in a World War I artillery battery, he had a relatively unsuccessful career in business, offset by camaraderie in a Masonic lodge, a Legion post, and civic clubs. He found his métier in politics but had to make his way as an honest man beholden to a corrupt machine. Handicapped also by shortness and extreme near-sightedness, he developed a style in which graciousness and good humor were combined with an appearance of quickness, tough self-assurance, and decisiveness. He carried this style to the Senate and then to the Presidency. As a onetime member of his staff observes, "He saw the President as man-in-charge of government. . . . His confidence was highest when he saw himself deciding and initiating. . . . Few things made him more uncomfortable than mulling over 'ifs' and 'buts' with nothing to decide." [44] Without venturing far into psychological analysis, one can hypothesize that if Truman had had to choose among adjectives to describe his action, he would have preferred "firm" to "flexible" and "bold" to "prudent." Such preferences influenced his behavior in 1950.

The logic of the Cold War provides another part of the answer. In Truman's eyes, the free world and the communist world faced one another as enemies poised for battle. The free world had adopted a dual strategy of containment and deterrence, the objectives being to prevent communist expansion pending that mellowing of the Soviet system which would permit live-and-let-live understandings and to instill in the communists such fear of their own destruction as to dissuade them from breaking the cordon around them by acts of war. The invasion of South Korea could be seen as jeopardizing the success of this strategy. On the one hand, it enlarged the communist domain, and, on the other hand, it put in question whether the free world was bluffing in the threat to counter violence with violence.

Truman saw the invasion in these terms. Since the lines of containment had not as yet been drawn so precisely in Asia as in Europe and the Middle East, the simple prospect of further minor expansion by the communists might not have alarmed him.[45] Less than a year had passed since the intelligence services had startled Truman with news that the Russians now had atomic bombs. During the winter of 1949–50 he had decided to speed work on the hydrogen bomb, the conclusive consideration having been apprehension that the Russians might already be developing such a weapon. Although Truman believed that the advantage in overall military power still lay with the United States and its allies, he did not know whether the Kremlin's estimates jibed with his. He had to fear that if the Soviets sensed any irresoluteness on the part of the United States, they might gamble on a military strike into Europe or the Middle East. Although experts on the Soviet Union told him that the Korean invasion appeared a limited move and that there were no signs of impending action elsewhere, Truman was not reassured. As he summarizes the rationale presented to Allied governments:

> It was essential to the maintenance of peace that this armed aggression against a free nation be met firmly. . . . Firmness now would be the only way to deter new actions in other portions of the world. Not only in Asia but in

> Europe, the Middle East, and elsewhere the confidence
> of peoples in countries adjacent to the Soviet Union would
> be very adversely affected . . . if we failed to take ac-
> tion to protect a country established under our auspices
> and confirmed in its freedom by action of the United
> Nations.[46]

Such reasoning can be traced in part to recent experience.
The passage in Truman's memoirs continues, "If . . . the
threat to South Korea was met firmly and successfully, it
would add to our successes in Iran, Berlin and Greece a
fourth success in opposition to the aggressive moves of the
Communists. And each success . . . was likely to add to the
caution of the Soviets in undertaking new efforts of this kind."
The abstract, almost mathematical logic of containment and
deterrence, however, could equally well have led him to the
position that he adopted.

Reinforcing the logic was concern about America's allies.
In 1949 the Truman administration had negotiated the North
Atlantic Treaty. Since the European parties were individually
and even collectively weaker than the Soviet Union, they required assurance that Americans would help them resist a
Russian attack. Otherwise, it was argued, they might see no
alternative to capitulation. Truman had reason to worry lest
these new partners lose confidence in the United States. As
Glenn Paige summarizes reports in the *New York Times,*

> heads of state turned to fix their inquiring gaze on Wash-
> ington. French eyes fearful for Indochina watched to
> see whether the United States would save its "Korean
> protégé" from destruction. The Cabinet of the Nether-
> lands came out of conference with a collective stare which
> apparently meant that ". . . it is up to the United
> States to take a hand in Korea or Western prestige will
> drop all over the world." [47]

When Harriman reached Washington, he told the President
that Europeans had been "gravely concerned lest we fail to
meet the challenge in Korea." They held, he said, that "dis-

aster would otherwise be certain." [48] Among possible consequences of not going to war in Korea, Truman could see not
only emboldenment of the Soviets but also a dissolution of
the barrier to their advance so painstakingly begun in Europe.
This latter consideration could have weighed heavily with
him.

Further, thoughts concerning domestic politics might have
influenced the President. To be sure, he prided himself on
not letting politics affect his management of foreign affairs,
and he rebuked Under Secretary Webb for bringing up the
subject at one of the Blair House conferences. Yet as Theodore
C. Sorenson writes, "Some Presidents may assert that they
are 'above politics,' yet politics, in its truest and broadest sense,
still colors their every decision (including the decision to
appear nonpolitical)." [49]

As of June 1950 Truman faced accelerating criticism on
account of the "loss" of China. Senator Joseph R. McCarthy
had recently blamed this and other unhappy events on the
presence of 205 or 81 or 57 card-carrying communists in the
State Department; and McCarthy's charges registered with
an extraordinarily large proportion of the citizenry: 86 per cent
knew about them, as opposed to 49 per cent who knew about
the defense-of-Taiwan issue.[50] Despite the Senate Republican
Policy Committee resolution saying that the United States had
no obligation to fight for South Korea, the President could
easily foresee that if South Korea were conquered, that fact
would be added to the bill of indictment against his administration. Polls asking whether the public approved or dis-
approved of his leadership had shown a decline in approval
from 69 per cent in January 1949 to 45 per cent in January
1950 to 37 per cent on the eve of the Korean crisis. His standing thus approached the earlier lows of October 1946 (32
per cent) and April 1948 (36 per cent) from which his popularity had recovered as a result, in the one instance, of the
Truman Doctrine and, in the other, of the airlift to Berlin.[51]

With the leadership in the Republican party rapidly shifting to those whom Acheson termed "the primitives" and with congressional elections only a little over four months away, Truman could have wanted to do the dramatic and profit from the all-for-one sentiment ordinarily accompanying a war. If so, he doubtless recognized the truth of Acheson's counsel that "we could not count on the continuance of the enthusiastic support that our staunch attitude in Korea had evoked. . . . Firm leadership would be less popular if it should involve casualties and taxes." [52] But his instincts could have told him that the emotion would persist at least through November.

Even taking account of Truman's personal style, the logic of containment and deterrence, signals coming from Europe, and domestic political considerations, one still cannot pull together a fully plausible explanation of why he acted as he did. His decisions themselves may become more explicable, but the manner of them does not. On the contrary, most of these factors add to one's puzzlement. For along with his relish for decision-making went a strong sense that the decision-maker needed facts and needed to hear all sides before rendering judgment.[53] His assertion at the first Blair House conference that he had an "open mind" and his assurance there to Webb that he would not take quick action betokened his view of how a President ought to behave. Especially since on two previous occasions he had decided that Korea had negligible value for the United States, his temperament should have led him to insist on convincing argumentation to prove the earlier position wrong.

The logic of containment and deterrence could have led Truman almost as easily to a conclusion opposite from the one he reached. Cunning Kremlin strategists, he could have assumed, were trying to entrap the United States. They had chosen ground where Americans would be at a disadvantage and where the Soviet Union, able to use the endless manpower of Asia, could fight with minimal cost and risk to itself. Further, he might have reasoned, they had selected a place where little was to be lost. Even if the United States fought and won, it would merely regain land admittedly of little value. Having achieved the defeat only of North Korea, it would score no gain in prestige. Truman could have estimated that the Soviets would be more, not less, likely to test the boundaries of containment or initiate war in Europe or the Middle East if they succeeded in pinning down American forces in a far-away corner of Asia.

As for the European allies, it was arguable that they would be more secure in mind and in fact—not less so—if assured that the United States had the wisdom not to waste its ready strength and reserves in a secondary area. That inklings of such arguments passed through Truman's head is evident in his persistent inquiries about Soviet activity elsewhere than Korea. Nevertheless, one gets the impression that Truman did not really open his mind to any argumentation or evidence counter to his initial impulse to "hit them hard."

It is wholly implausible that Truman thus shut his mind solely because instinct promised a short-run gain in domestic popularity. Since neither his general predispositions nor the logic of the terrifying international game in which he was engaged suffice for explanation, something else must have been determinative. As I read the record, that something else was Truman's set of beliefs about recent history.

Truman saw the 1930's as teaching a plain and unmistakable lesson. He knew much about earlier periods and sometimes referred to them. When encouraging the South Korean ambassador, he mentioned not only America's rescue of the Allies in 1917 but also Washington's recovery after Valley Forge. When approving withdrawal from Korea in 1949, he had thought— or so he recalled—of his Southern ancestors' eagerness for the end of Reconstruction.[54] But such analogies seldom seemed to have for him such force as those from the remembered decade prior to World War II.

As a freshman senator after 1934, Truman had voted with the majority that endorsed neutrality legislation. His memoirs suggest that he then found convincing the thesis that munitions makers and bankers had maneuvered the United States into mistakenly intervening in World War I.[55] Like many others, Truman experienced something like a conversion after Pearl Harbor. He felt shame and guilt for his earlier stand. He became utterly convinced that the League powers had acted wrongly in not combining to resist the first challenges to the Covenant by Japan, Italy, and Germany. He became equally convinced that the United States had been wrong not to arm itself and support or even lead in forcibly opposing aggression.

These convictions underpinned much of his thinking about international politics. In regard to international control of nuclear weapons, Truman did not think of the precedent of naval limitation treaties. As Baruch recalls:

> I pointed out that in the last analysis the only penalty we could invoke against a nation found guilty of transgression was war. Mr. Truman was absolutely firm on this. "I quite agree with you," he said. He went on to declare that if the world had followed Henry Stimson in his call for sanctions against Japan at the time she invaded Manchuria, the Second World War might never have occurred.[56]

When first brooding about the news of North Korea's attack, Truman's thoughts were chiefly about seeming analogues from the 1930's. Reminiscing, he writes of his flight from Independence to Washington:

> I had time to think aboard the plane. In my generation, this was not the first occasion when the strong had attacked the weak. I recalled some earlier instances: Manchuria, Ethiopia, Austria. I remembered how each time that the democracies failed to act it had encouraged the aggressors to keep going ahead. Communism was acting in Korea just as Hitler, Mussolini, and the Japanese

had acted ten, fifteen, and twenty years earlier. . . .
If this was allowed to go unchallenged it would mean a
third world war, just as similar incidents had brought on
a second world war.[57]

Elsewhere in his memoirs, Truman asserts, "I had trained my-
self to look back in history for precedents." When interviewed
by Glenn Paige in 1957, he reaffirmed "belief that the 'lessons
of history' offered clear guides to 'right principles' of action,"
and he said that he "weighed the North Korean invasion in
the balance of past experience." [58]

Talking with his advisers, Truman indicated his certainty
about the lesson taught by history. None of them questioned
his analysis. Indeed, they displayed agreement. At the first
Blair House conference, at least one other participant cited the
parallel of Japanese, Italian, and German aggression in the
1930's. At the second conference, according to Paige, everyone
agreed that "refusal to repel the aggression would be nothing
but 'appeasement.' And appeasement, as history has shown,
would ultimately lead to war." Rusk said in retrospect that the
government's decision had had little to do with Korea—it "was
in the process of being made for an entire generation since
Manchuria." [59]

Echoes from the press and especially from Capitol Hill
merely reinforced Truman's essential conviction. The newspapers he regularly read—the *Washington Post, Baltimore
Sun, New York Herald Tribune,* and *New York Times*—all
alluded in editorials to parallels from the 1930's. In the Senate
debate, Republicans Styles Bridges of New Hampshire, William
F. Knowland of California, and Alexander L. Wiley of Wisconsin did likewise. In the House, Republican Jacob Javits of
New York characterized the difference between the United
Nations and the League as "the difference . . . between Korea
and Ethiopia," and Democrat Abraham Ribicoff of Connecticut
declared, "What difference is there in the action of northern
Koreans today and the actions which led to the Second World

War? Talk about parallels!" [60] Truman was not alone in being certain that he understood the lessons of recent history; but it was his own certainty, probably, that determined his precipitancy in deciding for war.

Because of the earlier studies and decisions, evaluating Korea as of negligible importance and concluding that warfare there should be avoided, the 1950 decision provides a particularly vivid illustration of the potency of beliefs about history. When events in the peninsula were perceived as analogous to certain events in the recent past, an axiom derived from the analogies came into play, and all previous calculations lost their force.

Had the President been less cock-sure either about the lessons of history or about their applicability in the Korean case, he might have had more qualms. Had his advisers not recognized and shared his certitude, they might have taken more pains to assess the advantages and disadvantages of alternative courses.

Once again it has to be emphasized that no one can judge whether or not a different decision by Truman would have had happier consequences. Adam Ulam, probably the most dispassionate Western analyst of Soviet foreign policy, doubts that Stalin authorized the North Korean attack in order to test the willingness of the United States to defend Europe or the Middle East. Ulam surmises instead that Stalin interpreted American behavior in China as indicating that the United States had written off the Asian continent; hence he saw an opportunity for "an easy tidying-up operation." [61] Nevertheless, a quick success in Korea might have emboldened "hawks" in the Kremlin. Also, American failure to react might have prompted Japanese, Southeast Asians, and people elsewhere to conclude that safety lay in coming to terms with the communists. Events thus set in train might have brought the Soviet Union and the United States to an inescapable confrontation. Even at a remove of two decades, one cannot confidently second-guess Truman's decision.

Nor can one feel any assurance that the decision would have been different if Truman and the men around him had been more judicious in invoking history. Very little analysis by them would have been required to notice the many differences between conditions of the 1930's and those of 1950. Very little more would have been needed to set in the foreground recollection that control of Korea had been an aim of imperial Russia and that Stalin had consistently sought to fulfill the ambitions of the Tsars. With this history in mind, Truman and his advisers might have perceived that the communist action could be seen as not a first step in a new campaign of conquest but rather as a last move in an old campaign. Had they paused to think either about the aptness of the analogies they were invoking or about other historical data that might be pertinent, they might have recognized that an important element in their reasoning was faulty.

Their reasoning might nevertheless have brought them to the same conclusion. Even in this instance, where presumed lessons from a past episode appear to have had critical influence, the citation of history may have been part of a process of rationalization. In other words, Truman and others may have stressed the historical example because it confirmed a conviction to which they had been brought by some deeper, perhaps unconscious processes of mind, not because the example itself generated the conviction.

One has to ask why it was that Truman and so many of the men around him perceived the situation of the United States in 1950 as parallel to that of the Western democracies in the 1930's. One possible answer is that the actual points of parallel were so close as to force the comparison on them. A second is that the events of the 1930's had made a specially deep impression because they had themselves matured during the period. A third is that by equating the communists with the Nazis and invoking the conventional wisdom about the 1930's, they could find a moral justification for doing what they inwardly wanted to do because of their capitalist-imperialist ideology, their instinctive aggressive impulses, or something else which they preferred to keep buried.

These possible answers are not mutually exclusive. Certainly it was understandable that they should see parallels with the 1930's. There seemed no doubt that the Soviet Union had at least approved the North Korean attack. It was therefore reasonable to classify the event as a case of military aggression by a great power against a lesser power. The instances of the 1930's which Truman enumerated to himself were clearly major cases in the same category. While one can criticize the President and his advisers for thinking only of this category of experience, one cannot deny that there were enough elements of similarity to have made the comparisons inescapable.

It is also the case that the events of the 1930's had made a specially deep imprint on Truman and most of his associates. Sixty-two in 1950, the President himself was almost as old as Roosevelt would have been. He naturally remembered the debate about participation in the League of Nations. Issues of that period had not, however, had as much saliency for him as for Roosevelt. During World War II, he echoed what other leaders in his party were saying. In a speech in 1943, for example, Truman declared, "A small group of willful men kept us from assuming our world obligations in 1919–20, and the same thing can happen again. I am just as sure as I can be that this World War is the result of the 1919–20 isolationist attitude." [62] When coping with the responsibilities of the Presidency, his mind usually reverted, however, to events that had occurred after he became personally involved in national politics. Acheson, Louis Johnson, Rusk, Jessup, and others in the Truman circle had their first intellectual and emotional engagement with issues in international relations as a result of the succession of crises commencing in 1931. For all of these men, the 1930's was the most vivid period in history.

Even so, some hidden forces may have been at work in their

minds, bringing forward those half-remembered pieces of the past which best reinforced impulses to use power, gain greater power, and, in doing so, harm those who denied their creed. Thomas Lifka demonstrates that American officials had already developed a vocabulary which equated the Soviet Union with Fascist Italy and Nazi Germany. The word "totalitarian," previously applied only to the latter, had been enlarged in meaning to include Russia.[63] It may be that scarcely noticed adaptations of this sort were indicative of psychological processes of which the individuals themselves were unconscious. Such a hypothesis can be neither proved nor disproved. Still, it cannot be left wholly out of account.

Even with regard to the decision for intervention in Korea, where American statesmen appear to have discarded previous calculations because of a presumed maxim from history, more critical and systematic use of history might not have affected the outcome. Conceding this point, one can still assert that Truman and his advisers should have recognized the important role that historical evidence played in their reasoning. They should also have recognized that they were fixing on only one piece of history—and that a piece which had as yet been subjected to little detached examination. Had they noticed these characteristics of their thinking and tried to employ history more reflectively, the records of their deliberations might at least show that they had seriously analyzed alternatives before electing to spend life and sow destruction. This they did not do.

IV

Vietnam:
The Bed of Procrustes

After the first year of the Korean War, most of the history of American foreign policy is obscure. The congressional investigation of 1951, bringing to light much evidence about the intervention in Korea and the conduct of the war, was not to be duplicated. Although several studies have appeared of episodes in the Eisenhower administration, they rest on interview data, almost wholly unsupported by contemporary documents.[1] One may suspect that Eisenhower, his Secretary of State, John Foster Dulles, and others in the administration were just as prone as their Democratic predecessors to making uncritical use of analogies and historical trend-readings; but the evidence necessary for confirming or disproving this suspicion remains under lock and key. A little more is known about the Kennedy administration because of the President's tragic death and the subsequent publication of extensive, document-based biographies by Arthur M. Schlesinger, Jr., and Theodore C. Sorenson. In addition, there have appeared extraordinarily informative monographs on the Cuban missile crisis, based largely on interviews.[2] Even so, not enough records are open for research to permit close examination of how, if at all, precepts from history entered into policy.

The only decisions sufficiently documented are those of the Kennedy and Johnson administrations relating to Vietnam. This is the case because Secretary of Defense Robert McNamara ordered preparation of a documentary history of those decisions. Daniel Ellsberg, one of the men who worked on this highly classified history, elected to turn most of it over to the newspapers, and it subsequently appeared in print. On the basis of these volumes and the published recollections of participants, the reasoning behind American policy toward Vietnam in the early and mid-1960's can be provisionally reconstructed.

By this time, the American government had changed. The numbers of organizations and individuals dealing with national security affairs had greatly increased. The gathering of intelligence, the conduct of relations with other governments, and the processes of planning for diplomatic, military, or covert action had all become much more elaborate and sophisticated. For these reasons, it might be assumed that simplistic historical inferences had come to play a lesser part in policy-making. This was not the case.

When Kennedy became President in 1961, he faced problems in many areas abroad. Vietnam did not lead the list. After the French defeat there in 1954, a conference at Geneva had partitioned the country, with Ho Chi Minh setting up a communist-controlled state north of the seventeenth parallel, and non-communists putting together a government for the territory south of that line. At the time almost everyone assumed that the communists would soon take over all of the country. Surprisingly, this did not occur. Under President Ngo Dinh Diem, South Vietnam retained its independence. Supplied with large amounts of American aid, his regime even began to seem stable and hardy. Despite increasing guerrilla activity by the communist-led National Liberation Front, Diem was judged by Americans in Saigon to need only marginally greater American assistance in order to retain power. Kennedy therefore saw the need to decide how much the United States should contribute to South Vietnam and for what, but his choices chiefly concerned his budget, and he had to deal with many such issues.

Of far greater concern to the new President was Vietnam's neighbor Laos. There, the North Vietnamese had long supported a Pathet Lao group which from time to time had seemed on the verge of triumph. Clandestinely, American agencies had aided anti-communist factions. Just before Kennedy's inauguration, the Soviet government openly joined the North Vietnamese in supplying the Pathet Lao. Fleets of Soviet planes delivered weapons and equipment to landing fields in the sparsely settled Laotian highlands. Like Berlin, Laos became a place where the two super-powers stood fist to fist.

During the new administration's settling-in period, Laos temporarily took second place to Cuba. In that country, guerrillas had won power in 1959. Their leader, Fidel Castro, had then proclaimed himself a communist and established an alliance with the Soviet Union. Anti-communist Cuban refugees secured backing from the C.I.A. for plots against the Cuban regime, and Kennedy gave approval to a C.I.A. plan for landing refugee military units on the island. The operation, taking place at the Bay of Pigs, proved a fiasco. Kennedy publicly took the blame. Privately, he vowed in future to place less trust in advice and recommendations from the bureaucracy.

Returning to the Laotian problem, he pressed questions about the possible consequences of alternative courses of action. Some in his entourage advocated sending in American troops. Remembering vexedly that the Joint Chiefs of Staff had failed to warn him of what might happen at the Bay of Pigs, the President insisted that the chiefs spell out the possible consequences. He found them unwilling to give any assurance of success unless authorized to deploy large ground forces and, if necessary, use nuclear weapons.[3]

This counsel caused Kennedy to turn much more decidedly toward a course of action for which he had shown some inclination even during a pre-inauguration interview with Eisenhower. While leaving open the possibility of ordering troops into Laos, he bent his efforts toward negotiating a compromise. If the Laotian leaders could be brought into a coalition and if the United States and the Soviet Union both undertook to keep hands off, Laos would cease to be a battlefield of the Cold War and become instead a testing ground for a global armistice. So reasoning, Kennedy came to regard successful neutralization of Laos as an objective transcending most others.

It was with negotiations over Laos in the background that the Kennedy administration studied Vietnam. Reports from that country told of marked increases in guerrilla activity, and Americans on the scene expressed certainty not only that the North Vietnamese supplied and directed the guerrillas but that the new level of warfare reflected a conscious decision in Hanoi to bring down Diem and install a communist or communist-controlled government in Saigon. Warned that the North Vietnamese might well succeed, Kennedy faced the question of whether or not to commit the United States to preventing Diem's fall.

The President and his advisers appreciated the gravity of the issue. Although an American military advisory group functioned in Saigon and almost four billion dollars in economic and military aid had been contributed to South Vietnam since 1954, the fate of the country still depended in large part on the South Vietnamese themselves. If the communists won, Washington could say that the United States had done as much as a distant friendly power could, but that Diem had proved incapable of enlisting the loyalty of his people. If, on the other hand, Americans assumed a direct role in combating the guerrillas, a victory for the communists would seem more a defeat for the United States.

In the early autumn of 1961, Kennedy sent to Vietnam two members of the White House staff, General Maxwell Taylor and former M.I.T. professor Walt Rostow. Taylor, once chief of staff of the army, had been added to Kennedy's entourage after the Bay of Pigs as an independent adviser on military questions. Upon return, Taylor and Rostow recommended:

1. A quick U.S. response to the present crisis which would demonstrate by deeds—not merely words—the American commitment seriously to help save Vietnam rather than to disengage in the most convenient manner possible. To be persuasive this commitment must include the sending to Vietnam of some U.S. military forces.
2. A shift in the American relation to the Vietnamese effort from advice to limited partnership.[4]

Cables to diplomatic and military missions in Asia, memoranda exchanged in Washington, and a number of face-to-face meetings in the Pentagon, State Department, C.I.A., and White House assessed the pros and cons of these recommendations. Secretary of Defense McNamara, an energetic, self-confident, and analytically brilliant former president of the Ford Motor Company, reported to the President that, if the Taylor-Rostow recommendations were followed and if the North Vietnamese and even possibly the Chinese were to respond in kind, the United States might have to deploy as many as 205,000 troops. "To accept the stated objective," observed McNamara, "is . . . a most serious decision."[5]

Kennedy's Secretary of State was Dean Rusk. Having spent some of his World War II army service in the China-Burma-India theater and having been Assistant Secretary of State for Far Eastern Affairs during the final years of the Truman administration, he had kept up with news from Asia. More than most of his colleagues, or for that matter most Foreign Service officers, he recognized the apparent solidity of the Diem regime as a possible illusion. Absent on an official trip at the time when Taylor and Rostow delivered their report, he cabled the President, "While attaching greatest possible importance to security in SEA [Southeast Asia], I would be reluctant to see U.S. make major additional commitment American prestige to a losing horse." [6]

Viewed simply in the circumstances of 1961, the arguments against the Taylor-Rostow recommendations were mostly summed up in Rusk's comment and in an appraisal prepared in Honolulu by the staff of the Commander-in-Chief, Pacific.[7] The Diem government might prove to have no staying power. American troops might be seen by the Vietnamese as agents of a new colonial power, threatening their independence. If so, the insurgents could gain strength. In any case, the North Vietnamese and perhaps the Chinese would have a valid pretext for stepping up support of the communists or perhaps intervening themselves. Americans would inevitably become involved in counter-guerrilla operations for which they were ill-prepared, and large numbers might be so engaged for a long period of time.

In terms of factors immediately in play, the arguments for adopting the Taylor-Rostow recommendations were more complex. If the North Vietnamese were to win control over South Vietnam, the likelihood of their accepting any compromise in Laos would probably disappear, no matter what might be the disposition of the Soviet Union. Laos could not then serve as a test of possibilities for a broader American-Soviet détente. Many people in the American government thought a Laotian settlement unlikely in any case, and communist takeover of Laos probable. On these assumptions, it could be contended that the United States ought to make a stand in Vietnam in order to prove that willingness to negotiate about Laos did not signify willingness to abandon all of Southeast Asia.

It could further be argued that, if Laos and South Vietnam

both came under communist domination, Cambodia, Thailand, Burma, Malaya, and Indonesia would quickly follow suit. Speaking of the countries of Southeast Asia, Eisenhower had once used the simile of a row of standing dominoes. At the time, Democrats criticized his figure of speech. When asked about the so-called "domino theory," Kennedy responded, however, "I believe it. I believe it." [8]

Were communists or their sympathizers to take over all or most of Southeast Asia, it was held, China and the Soviet Union would achieve a major gain in the Cold War. When avowing his faith in the domino theory, Kennedy had explained, "China is so large, looms so high just beyond the frontiers, that if South Viet-Nam went, it would not only give them an improved geographic position . . . but would also give the impression that the wave of the future in Southeast Asia was China and the Communists." Always militant in rhetoric, the Chinese leaders had recently deployed troops to install a protégé in Tibet, conducted skirmishes on the Indian frontier, and offered military "volunteers" to help President Sukarno suppress a revolt in Indonesia. With a large army, the world's third-ranking air force, and a crash program under way for development of nuclear weapons, China seemed likely soon to have strength for even more adventurous moves. And most observers could not yet credit evidence of Chinese-Soviet antagonism. In any case, Kennedy was to remark in a 1963 speech that "hope must be tempered with caution. For the Soviet-Chinese disagreement is over means, not ends." [9]

Analyzing the scene as of 1961, men around the President could argue for putting troops in Vietnam to conserve hope of an American-Soviet agreement on Laos, to have an advanced position in Southeast Asia in case such an agreement did not materialize, to demonstrate to Thai leaders and others that, in spite of seeking to neutralize Laos, the United States would support non-communist governments in the region, and above all, to hold a line against the aggressive advance of the Chinese. These were, in fact, the contentions at the core of memoranda advising a military commitment in Vietnam.

In the end every member of Kennedy's inner circle supported such a commitment. Despite his earlier words of caution, Rusk joined McNamara in recommending to the President that "We now take the decision to commit ourselves to the objective of preventing the fall of South Viet-Nam to Communism and that, in doing so, we recognize that the introduction of United States . . . forces may be necessary to achieve this objective." [10] The formula which the secretaries proposed and the President accepted involved dispatch of several thousand soldiers, but with instructions at the outset to serve only as advisers to Diem's commanders and administrators. Although their engaging in combat against the guerrillas seemed almost inevitable, Kennedy could forbear giving orders to such effect and thus leave open some limited opportunity for later reconsideration. At the time, however, he and the men around him clearly saw the arguments for fighting in Vietnam as much more compelling than those against.

Although the principal items in this balance sheet concerned current conditions and future prospects, beliefs about the past entered into the weighings and the tallies.

With varying degrees of precision, every participant in the debate remembered France's experiences in Indo-China. In the spring of 1961 when the new administration first examined Diem's pleas for more help, a State Department memorandum commented that the French commitment had run to 200,000 men. Probably this reminder traced to Deputy Under Secretary George Ball, who had represented the French government as a lawyer during the last year of its humiliating effort to hold the colony.[11] After the Taylor-Rostow report became the focus of discussion, Deputy Assistant Secretary of Defense William P. Bundy was a principal adviser to McNamara. Earlier, Bundy had spent ten years in the C.I.A., working chiefly on broad estimates of current and future trends. He offered an opinion, "based on very close touch with Indochina in the 1954 war and civil war afterwards till Diem took hold," which said that "an early and hard-hitting operation has a good chance (70% would be my guess) of *arresting* things and giving Diem a chance to do better and clean up. . . . The 30% chance is that we would wind up like the French in 1954; white men can't win this kind of fight." [12]

Harvard economics professor John Kenneth Galbraith, whom Kennedy had appointed ambassador to India, sent the President the only emphatic recommendation against committing American troops to Vietnam. Warning of the administration's "bright promise being sunk under the rice fields," Galbraith urged Kennedy to remember that Eisenhower and Secretary of State John Foster Dulles had decided not to risk an effort to rescue the French after their calamitous defeat at Dienbienphu. "Dulles in 1954," he remarked, "saw the dangers in this area." [13]

Kennedy himself had taken a special interest in Indo-China as a member of the House and Senate in the early 1950's. He had even had his French-speaking wife, Jacqueline, translate reading matter for him.[14] As with Ball and William Bundy, recollection of what had befallen the French probably entered his thoughts as an important count against committing American soldiers.

To some extent, memories of the Korean War produced a similar effect. Although almost no one questioned the correctness and courageousness of Truman's decision to fight that war, everyone in the government recalled that early United Nations victories, including a march deep into North Korea, had been followed by Chinese intervention. Hard fighting had dragged on for two years, taken over 54,000 American lives, and left more than 100,000 others wounded or in captivity. Moreover, the war had divided the public. On the one hand, millions had clamored for bombing or blockading of China in spite of the

Truman administration's estimate that such actions could lead to an all-out war with the Soviet Union. On the other hand, quieter millions had evidenced impatience with continuing casualty reports and economic controls and appeared willing to see the war ended on almost any terms. Public approval of Truman, as measured by Gallup polls, fell as low as 23 per cent.[15] Promises by Eisenhower that he would bring peace played a part in his 6.6 million-vote margin, and the actual armistice in 1953, even though involving some concessions to the communists, was greeted with relieved approval throughout the country.

These experiences were thought to convey two lessons. First, they confirmed that the United States should never fight a land war in Asia. Second, they demonstrated that the American people had little stomach for a prolonged, limited war.

Available documents on the Vietnam debate of 1961 contain few references to the Korean War and its alleged lessons. Since documents of 1964 and later contain many, this fact is surprising. The probable explanation is that the debate over Laos had made men sensitive about mentioning Korea. Roger Hilsman's retrospective account of that debate suggests why. Then head of the State Department's Bureau of Intelligence and Research, Hilsman was a former Columbia University political science professor and one of the cluster of intellectuals and academics close to the throne. He believed the Joint Chiefs to have exaggerated when they estimated requirements for intervention in Laos. He writes,

> it was a shibboleth among the Joint Chiefs of Staff that the United States ought never again to fight a limited war on the ground in Asia. . . . Some who held this view —among the staff of the JCS and even among the JCS themselves—seemed suspicious that even a show of force in Asia might be a White House or State Department plot to trap them into a situation where a limited war could not be avoided. . . . Not all of the Joint Chiefs fully subscribed to the "Never Again" view, but it seemed to the

White House that they were at least determined to build a record that would protect their position and put the blame entirely on the President no matter what happened.[16]

Feeling that the "lessons" of Korea might be exaggerated by the military, civilians in the administration refrained from touching on them. Doubtless aware that they were suspected of timidity, the careerists did likewise. Further, as Hilsman relates, some "never again" sentiment appeared in the press and in Congress.[17]

On occasion, advisers to the President alluded to widespread fears of a ground war in Asia. When urging firm support of Diem, Vice President Lyndon Johnson mentioned as one problem "the extent that fear of ground troop involvement dominates our political responses to Asia in Congress or elsewhere." [18] When Taylor recommended the dispatch of military advisers, he took pains to say, "The risks of backing into a major Asian war . . . are present but not impressive." Describing North Vietnam as "extremely vulnerable to conventional bombing," Taylor forecast that both the North Vietnamese and the Chinese "would face severe logistical difficulties in trying to maintain strong forces in the field. . . . There is no case for fearing a mass onslaught of Communist manpower." [19] Probably, the President and most of his advisers refrained from invoking the alleged lessons of Korea because, in the first place, they regarded them as too well understood to require mention and in the second place, because they suspected that any such reference would concede a point to the military. Even so, the Korean example undoubtedly remained at the back of their minds, warning against a war in Vietnam.

On the other hand, analogies from experience elsewhere in Asia seemed to argue in favor of military action by the United States. A few years after World War II, communist-led insurgents had developed strength in both the Philippine Islands and Malaya. By deploying small, specially trained military units, policing secured areas, confining captured rebels in isolated reconcentration camps, curbing corruption, and improving public services, Ramon Magsaysay and his associates regained almost complete control of the Philippines. In Malaya, British and native forces cut off supplies, rounded up rebels, and resettled them in controlled areas. Both cases were taken by American officials as demonstrating that relatively specialized small-scale military operations, coupled with positive measures of other types, could overcome guerrillas. These cases suggested that an effort different from and below that of the Korean War could yield success in Vietnam.

In 1961 President Kennedy and his intimates tended to see Vietnam much more in the image of the Philippines and Malaya than in that of Korea. According to Arthur Schlesinger, Jr., Kennedy's own judgment was that Magsaysay's campaign in the Philippines provided a model for Vietnam—"tough counter-guerrilla action, generous provisions for amnesty, real and sweeping reforms." [20] The President and his younger brother, Attorney General Robert F. Kennedy, superintended creation by the army of elite Special Forces trained for counter-guerrilla operations. They even selected headgear and shoes for these units.[21] And White House representatives criticized the army high command for thinking in Korean War terms and through its advisory mission preparing South Vietnam to fight a war like that of 1950–53. Instead, the chief of staff was told, the army should be thinking of a Malayan-style campaign.

While denying that army planning was as charged, the chief of staff paused to tick off five reasons why the Vietnamese and Malayan situations were not comparable:

a. Malayan borders were far more controllable. . . .
b. The racial characteristics of the Chinese insurgents in Malaya made identification and segregation a relatively

simple matter as compared with the situation in Vietnam. . . .
  c. The scarcity of food in Malaya versus the relative
     plenty in South Vietnam made the denial of food to
     the guerrillas a far more important and readily usable
     weapon in Malaya.
  d. Most importantly, in Malaya the British were in actual
     command. . . .
  e. Finally, it took the British nearly 12 years to defeat
     an insurgency that was less strong than the one in
     South Vietnam.[22]

It does not appear, however, that such analysis had any impact in the White House or for that matter among civilians
in the Defense Department or the State Department. As late
as 1964 McNamara was to cite Malaya as a precedent for
Vietnam, and Rusk in the same year was to recommend
Magsaysay as the example to be copied by South Vietnam's
president.[23]

If leaders of the Kennedy administration viewed Vietnam
itself as analogous to Malaya and the Philippines, they saw it
as symbolically akin to China. They remembered Republican
charges that the Democrats had "lost" China as having harmed
their party for a decade. That they believed the wellsprings
of public emotion to remain unchanged had been indicated by
Kennedy's efforts in the 1960 campaign to pin the blame for
"losing" Cuba on the Republicans. When advising the President to accept the Taylor-Rostow recommendations, Rusk and
McNamara stressed that "loss of South Vietnam would stimu-
late bitter domestic controversies in the United States and
would be seized upon by extreme elements to divide the
country and harass the Administration." [24] Explaining publicly
in 1963 all his efforts to shore up the South Vietnamese, Kennedy said, "Strongly in our mind is what happened in the case
of China at the end of World War II, where China was lost.
. . . We don't want that." [25] Although members of the admin-

istration seldom made such explicit admissions, it seems almost beyond doubt that recollection of congressional and public outcries about the "loss" of China cast a shadow whenever the possibility of abandoning the South Vietnamese flickered through their thoughts.

Finally, a commitment to defend South Vietnam was made to seem necessary and almost inevitable by the historical framework of the issue, as it was conventionally portrayed. Careerists repeatedly told the newly arrived political appointees that the communists had a plan for the conquest of the world and that their action in Vietnam was a calculated strategic move. The Joint Chiefs asserted to the Secretary of Defense and the President:

> It is recognized that the military and political effort of Communist China in South Vietnam . . . is part of a major campaign to extend communist control beyond the periphery of the Sino-Soviet bloc and overseas to both island and continental areas in the Free World. . . . It is, in fact, a planned phase in the communist timetable for world domination.[26]

In the State Department, the premier careerist and expert on Southeast Asia was Deputy Under Secretary U. Alexis Johnson. With twenty-five years in the Foreign Service, he had been in Japan with Grew and, after the war, with MacArthur, he was Rusk's deputy in the Far Eastern bureau during the Korean War; and most recently he had been ambassador to Thailand. Alexis Johnson believed that the communist design for taking over Southeast Asia dated back before World War II, and he had a hand in drafting the earliest analysis of the Vietnam problem submitted to the President. This document warned that "turmoil . . . throughout the area . . . provides an ideal environment for the Communist 'master plan' to take over all of Southeast Asia." [27] The long Taylor-Rostow report, partially drafted by careerists acting as staff assistants, said, "the Communists are pursuing a clear and systematic strategy in Southeast Asia." [28]

This representation of the historical background probably had some effect on the calculations of Kennedy and his advisers. To be sure, they were predisposed to view communism as an expanding and aggressive force. They also regarded all countries not allied with either the Soviet Union or the United States as battlegrounds in a global struggle between the two. These conceptions were widely shared. They permeated most American commentary on international politics, including that by scholars. During 1960 and 1961, the government and much of the press displayed concern lest communists gain the upper hand in the former Belgian Congo. It would not have been easy for members of the Kennedy administration to see Southeast Asia as anything but a battlefront in the Cold War.

In any case, the President's decision was to prevent the "loss" of Vietnam. Soon American military advisers were interlaced into the South Vietnamese command, down even to the platoon level, and American helicopter crews ferried Vietnamese soldiers and spotted targets for their artillery.

Despite increasing American aid and involvement, the likelihood of South Vietnam's falling to the communists seemed to grow. The guerrillas became more numerous and more bold, and North Vietnamese reinforcement of them at least matched American reinforcement of Saigon. By late 1964 actual North Vietnamese combat units had entered the south.

Increasingly, American observers saw reason to fear the Saigon regime's dissolution. Diem's administration reportedly became both more arbitrary and more corrupt. Non-communist groups demonstrated against it. American officials felt obliged to utter public reproach. Army leaders then effected a coup, overthrowing Diem and arranging for him to be murdered. Subsequently, one group of generals or politicians succeeded another, with no individual emerging as anything more than a factional leader.

Lyndon Johnson, who had become President after Kennedy's assassination, inherited the question of what to do about the worsening situation in Vietnam. To some extent, he faced the same choice as his predecessor. It remained open to him to wash his hands of Vietnam or, alternatively, to commit the United States to preventing communist victory. For Johnson, however, the former choice appeared much less attractive because of the extent to which Kennedy had already engaged American prestige. At the same time, it was more obvious that the second choice would involve heavy costs, for Johnson's advisers told him almost from the beginning that success might require bombing North Vietnam and ordering substantial American forces into combat in South Vietnam. In effect, Johnson had to decide whether or not to go to war.

Considerations on one side or the other were much like those of 1961. Recent events in Saigon argued for disengagement, for they made it seem more questionable than ever that South Vietnam deserved to be termed "free." Also, they increased significantly the chances of failure. Further, the possibility that the American public might not support a war in Vietnam had become far more apparent. Although polls, editorial commentary, and congressional votes all gave emphatic support to each militant step which the President actually took, disinclination to see American lives expended in Southeast Asia manifested itself when questioners at press conferences and congressional hearings asked sharply whether American advisers participated in combat. It also found expression in the election campaign of 1964, when Johnson defeated his bellicose Republican opponent, Barry Goldwater, by a margin of sixteen million votes. And in early 1965, when the President approached decisions for war, significant numbers of Congressmen and editorial writers voiced opposition.[29]

Domestically, the arguments against war rose not only from the possibility of its being unpopular but also from the near certainty that its costs would make more difficult the funding of various social welfare programs to which Johnson had a deep commitment. The 1964 elections also brought increases in the Democratic majorities in Congress. Using the persuasive skills which he had perfected as majority leader in the Senate, Johnson planned to press enactment of a number of major reforms. Many would entail new spending, and the President could see that, while the two houses might pass his bills, they would be more resistant to putting up the necessary money if at the same time they had to appropriate billions for a war in Southeast Asia.

The analytical arguments in favor of war had much more to do with what might happen outside the United States if the war were not fought. As compared with 1961, the reasoning remained practically unchanged. It was summarized succinctly in a National Security Action Memorandum endorsed by Johnson in March 1964:

> We seek an independent non-Communist South Vietnam. . . .
>
> Unless we can achieve this objective . . . almost all of Southeast Asia will probably fall under Communist dominance (all of Vietnam, Laos, and Cambodia), accommodate to Communism so as to remove effective U.S. and anti-Communist influence (Burma), or fall under the domination of forces not now explicitly Communist but likely then to become so (Indonesia taking over Malaysia). Thailand might hold for a period without help, but would be under grave pressure. Even the Philippines would become shaky, and the threat to India on the West, Australia and New Zealand to the South, and Taiwan, Korea, and Japan to the North and East would be greatly increased.[30]

Beyond the immediate region, it was feared, Vietnam might be taken as a test of American resoluteness and of the integrity of other American commitments. To withdraw, said Secretary Rusk, "would mean not only grievous losses to the free world in Southeast and southern Asia but a drastic loss of confidence in the will and capacity of the free world to oppose aggression." [31] Specifically, Rusk and others were concerned lest the NATO states and other American allies find reason for questioning whether the United States would actually come to their defense.

Were the communists to succeed in Vietnam, members of the administration believed, the Soviet Union and China would be inspired to stir up new insurgencies. In January 1961 Khrushchev had applauded "wars of national liberation." Many read this statement as proclaiming a new communist strategy and declaring Vietnam its first serious trial. Rusk said, "If Hanoi and Peiping prevail in Viet-nam in this key test of the new communist tactics of 'wars of national liberation,' then the Communists will use this technique with growing frequency elsewhere in Asia, Africa, and Latin America." [32]

As in 1961, so in 1964–65 debate involved not only calculations concerning present and future but also inferences from historical experience. The possible parallel with pre-1954 France continued to provoke doubts. It was very much in the mind of George Ball, now Under Secretary of State, who stood as the one convinced and consistent opponent of further military action. It also entered the thoughts of William Bundy, now the Assistant Secretary of State for Far Eastern Affairs, and John T. McNaughton, a Harvard law professor recruited by McNamara to replace Bundy as Assistant Secretary of Defense for International Security Affairs. The two men guided intensive staff work on Vietnam from the autumn of 1964 to the summer of 1965, and McNaughton once spoke of a "French-defeat syndrome" as an obstacle to detached consideration of large-scale troop deployments. [33]

The parallel had enough persuasiveness so that those who favored war felt some compulsion to argue its invalidity. McNamara offered public assurances that the two situations were not comparable, and a spokesman for the Joint Chiefs protested to William Bundy in November 1964:

> French errors . . . included major political delays and
> indecisions, which amongst other things tolerated if not
> enforced a military fiasco. Rather than now lamely resur-
> recting the story of how the French couldn't do the job,
> it seems to me we should instead make sure we don't re-
> peat their mistakes. (The French also tried to build the
> Panama Canal.)[34]

More powerful still was the possible parallel with the
Korean War. In specific ways, it had some effect on almost
everyone. The thought that some action by the United States
might provoke massive Chinese intervention, as had the
United Nations invasion of North Korea, entered almost every
discussion of possible action against North Vietnam. As it happened, the new chief of State's Bureau of Intelligence and
Research was Allen S. Whiting. In private life, he had written a book on China's intervention in Korea. By calling the
attention of his colleagues to every signal even faintly resembling ones heard in the autumn of 1950, he contributed
to keeping that particular experience alive in men's minds.[35]
Even the Joint Chiefs hedged their recommendation for bombing North Vietnam by noting that "there is a fair chance that
Peiping would introduce limited numbers of Chinese ground
forces as 'volunteers.'"[36] Similarly, some who yearned for a
negotiated solution somehow freeing the United States from
its dilemma expressed the view that the government should
not get entrapped, as it had in the Korean War, into talking
while the enemy continued to fight.[37]

In broad outline as well as in detail, the Korean parallel
preoccupied planners in the State Department. In a draft
paper for the National Security Council, Assistant Secretary
Bundy wrote,

> we cannot guarantee to maintain a non-Communist South
> Viet-Nam short of committing ourselves to whatever de-
> gree of military action would be required to defeat North
> Viet-Nam and probably Communist China militarily. Such
> a commitment . . . could not be confined to air and naval

action but would almost inevitably involve a Korean-scale
ground action and possibly even the use of nuclear
weapons at some point.[38]

Uncomfortable with all the options they could discern, the
officials thinking about Vietnam gravitated toward the idea of
going to war by escalating stages. The United States would
do some bombing in North Vietnam. This would demonstrate
American determination to persevere. If the communists did
not desist, the bombing would intensify and spread to new
targets. The question of introducing ground troops could be
faced somewhat later. The planners came to refer to this
scheme as "the slow squeeze." Although William Bundy saw
merits in it, he observed that:

> This course of action is inherently likely to stretch out
> and to be subject to major pressures both within the
> U.S. and internationally. As we saw in Korea, an "in-
> between" course of action will always arouse a school of
> thought that believes things should be tackled quickly and
> conclusively. On the other side, the continuation of mili-
> tary action and a reasonably firm posture will arouse sharp
> criticism in other political quarters.[39]

In a memorandum to Rusk, McNamara, and other presidential
advisers, Bundy addressed the question of whether "the slow
squeeze" could be "carried out in practice under the klieg
lights of a democracy." He commented, "This is a key point.
. . . The parallel to Korea in 1951–53 is forbidding." [40]

Rusk, whose memories of that period were full and vivid,
felt similar concern. At one point, he said to one of South
Vietnam's transitory heads of government that the United
States "would never again get involved in a land war in Asia
limited to conventional forces." [41] Down to the last moment,
he expressed qualms about "the slow squeeze," saying "that
the consequences of both escalation and withdrawal are so
bad that we simply must find a way of making our present
policy work." [42]

McNaughton referred to the "Korea syndrome" as another obstacle to stepped-up warfare, and the Joint Chiefs felt impelled to argue explicitly that the parallel was invalid.[43] If they had earlier been gripped by fear of reliving that war, they were not any longer. American troops had gone into action, albeit as advisers. Officers in Washington, Honolulu, and Saigon had worked out detailed plans for winning in Vietnam, and the chiefs were now intent only on obtaining from their political superiors a signal to proceed at full speed. Their expressed reservations had to do not with going to war but with going to war in stages. They advocated a "fast squeeze." In response to William Bundy's prediction of Korean-scale ground action, their representative commented,

> Our first objective is to cause the DRV [North Vietnam] to terminate support of the SEA [Southeast Asian] insurgencies. . . . To achieve this objective does not necessarily require that we "defeat North Viet-Nam," and it almost certainly does not require that we defeat Communist China. Hence our commitment to SVN [South Vietnam] does not involve a high probability . . . of a major conflict in Southeast Asia. . . . Certainly, no responsible person proposes to go about such a war, if it should occur, on a basis remotely resembling Korea. "Possibly even the use of nuclear weapons at some point" is of course why we spend billions to have them.

The chiefs did not address the possibility that domestic reactions might parallel those of the Korean War. One of their representatives came closest to doing so when noting, chiefly in reference to probable foreign criticism, that "We recognize quite clearly that any effective military action taken by the United States will generate a hue and cry in various quarters. The influence that this kind of 'pressure' may have upon the United States will be no more than what we choose to permit it to be." [44]

While recollections of the Korean War fuelled doubt, they also, paradoxically, encouraged boldness. Every participant in the governmental debate looked back with admiration at Truman's 1950 decision. Together with his decisions to defend Greece and Berlin and to create NATO, they believed, the intervention in Korea had demonstrated America's willingness to risk war in order to protect the integrity of other nations. They wanted to act in Vietnam in keeping with Truman's example.

This theme ran through all the debates of 1964 and 1965. Adlai Stevenson, then ambassador to the United Nations, said publicly in the summer of 1964, "The point is the same in Vietnam today as it was in Greece in 1947 and in Korea in 1950." [45] President Johnson himself declared during the same summer, "The challenge that we face in southeast Asia today is the same challenge that we have faced with courage and that we have met with strength in Greece and Turkey, in Berlin and Korea." [46]

In a ruminative draft memorandum, McNaughton wrote:

It is essential—however badly SEA [Southeast Asia] may go over the next 2–4 years—that U.S. emerge as a "good doctor." We must have kept promises, been tough, taken risks, gotten bloodied, and hurt the enemy very badly. We must avoid appearances which will affect judgments by, and provide pretexts to, other nations regarding U.S. power, resolve and competence. . . . The questions will be:

a. Has U.S. policy of containment against overt and covert aggression changed, at least as to SEA? How will we behave in new confrontations à la South Vietnam, Korea (1950), Berlin? . . .

b. Is U.S. *power* to contain insufficient, at least at the fringes?

c. Is the U.S. *hobbled by restraints* which might be relevant in future cases (fear of illegality, of U.N. or neutral reaction, of domestic pressures, of U.S. losses, of deploying U.S. ground forces in Asia, of war with China or Russia, of use of nuclear weapons, etc.)?[47]

When intensively studying the problem during the autumn, McNaughton and William Bundy explored alternatives to war. In doing so, they groped for ways of distinguishing a decision on Vietnam from the 1950 decision on Korea. A document jointly composed described the following as part of a fall-back position: "To make clear to the world, and to nations in Asia particularly, that failure in South Vietnam, if it comes, was due to special local factors—such as a bad colonial heritage and a lack of will to defend itself—that do not apply to other nations." [48] Amplifying the point, Bundy wrote,

> The honest fact is that South Viet-Nam and Laos have not really been typical cases from the beginning, which accounts in part for our inability to enlist the kind of international support we had in Korea and for our having to carry the load so largely alone. Most of the world had written off both countries in 1954, and our ability to keep them going—while an extraordinary and praiseworthy effort—has never given them quite the standing of such long-established national entities as Greece, Turkey, and Iran, or the special ward-of-the-U.N. status that South Korea had in 1950.[49]

Taking the lead in opposition to war, George Ball attacked the Korean analogy very much as the chairman of the Joint Chiefs had earlier attacked comparisons between South Vietnam and Malaya. Writing to Rusk, McNamara, and McGeorge Bundy, he ticked off points of dissimilarity between the situation facing Johnson and that which had faced Truman in 1950. "South Viet-Nam is not Korea," he declared, "and in making fundamental decisions it would be a mistake for us to rely too heavily on the Korean analogy."

First, Ball noted, intervention in Korea had express sanction from the United Nations. Second, the United States had, as a result, active support from other countries, including fifty-three that contributed troops. "In Viet-Nam," he observed, "we are going it alone." Third, South Korea had a stable government. South Vietnam by contrast exemplified "governmental chaos." Fourth, the South Koreans were newly independent and willing to fight for their nation. Having been at war for twenty years, the South Vietnamese had no such energy or sense of commitment. Ball concluded,

> Finally, the *Korean War* started with a massive land invasion by 100,000 troops. This was a classical type of invasion across an established border. . . . It gave us an unassailable political and legal base for counteraction.
>
> In South Viet-Nam there has been no invasion—only a slow infiltration. . . . The . . . insurgency does have substantial indigenous support. Americans know that the insurgency is actively directed and supported by Hanoi, but the rest of the world is not so sure. . . . And, as the weakness of the Saigon government becomes more and more evident, an increasing number of governments will be inclined to believe that the . . . insurgency is, in fact, an internal rebellion.[50]

Neither the Joint Chiefs nor Ball succeeded, however, in stripping the Korean example of its force. It was subsequently to be cited time and again both in internal memoranda and in public statements.

While Korea figured much more in the debate of 1964–65 than in that of 1961, the Philippine and Malayan analogies no longer did. McNaughton once mused that perhaps some Vietnamese leader might achieve an unexpected turn-around in public opinion such as Magsaysay had effected in the Philippines.[51] In general, however, officials tended simply to make passing mention of these earlier Southeast Asian cases as evidence that communist guerrillas could be defeated.

Officials now cited as seemingly stronger evidence the instance of Greece after American aid commenced in 1947. Perhaps Greece drew such notice because the Greek insurgents had had support from outside. Perhaps it was because the insurgency there had died down in two years instead of ten or twelve. In any case, many people mentioned it or thought of it. Henry Cabot Lodge, the ambassador in Saigon, did so. So did William Bundy, who had worked for the Greek government as a lawyer during the very period of its success against the guerrillas. Walt Rostow, now head of the State Department's Policy Planning Council, contributed the observation that if the United States used its military power with determination, "The odds are pretty good . . . that . . . we will see the same kind of fragmentation of the Communist movement in South Viet Nam that we saw in Greece." [52]

Arguing for ground force deployments as well as bombing, Rostow even offered what purported to be a systematic analysis of past guerrilla wars. Citing not only Greece, the Philippines, and Malaya but also Ireland after World War I, China, North Vietnam in the 1950's, and Laos, he argued that such wars nearly always ended in clear-cut victory or defeat. At some point, he alleged, the guerrillas usually commanded most of the countryside. Often they menaced the capital. When they won, it was by all-out conventional war (China), a political take-over (North Vietnam), a coalition settlement which permitted eventual take-over (Eastern Europe, rather than any of the cases supposedly under the microscope), or a partition arrangement (North Vietnam again, Laos, and Ireland). All the United States had to do, Rostow proffered, was to ensure that all these routes to communist victory remained closed.[53] As of 1964, however, Rostow had only a fugitive role in the debate. Everyone knew that he had been urging war against North Vietnam for years. Neither his enthusiasm for such a course, his optimism about its prospects, nor his opinion of the special relevance of previous guerrilla wars was widely shared.

How significant memories of public reaction to the fall of China remained is hard to estimate. In available documents, one finds only faint allusions. The last comprehensive analysis of policy options prior to the President's first critical decision was made by William Bundy's younger brother, McGeorge

Bundy, a former Harvard dean who had come to Washington
with Kennedy and remained to work for Johnson, occupying
throughout the crucial post of Special Assistant to the President for National Security Affairs. Often the last man to review an issue for the President, he had influence at least equal
to that of McNamara and Rusk. Johnson had sent Bundy and
McNamara in person for a last look around in South Vietnam,
and Bundy reported that he and the Secretary of Defense both
favored bombing North Vietnam. He continued,

> We . . . cannot estimate the odds of success with any
> accuracy—they may be somewhere between 25% and 75%.
> What we can say is that even if it fails, the policy will be
> worth it. At a minimum it will damp down the charge
> that we did not do all that we could have done, and this
> charge will be important in many countries, including
> our own.[54]

In retrospect, we can see that when ranking the arguments
for war in Vietnam President Johnson placed this consideration high on his list, second only to the danger that the rest
of Southeast Asia would fall. "A divisive debate about 'who
lost Vietnam' would be," he was to write, ". . . even more
destructive to our national life than the argument over China
had been." [55]

Deliberations about what the United States should do in
Vietnam were probably also influenced by the alleged lessons
of the 1930's. After examining all the options, the President
decided to proceed with "the slow squeeze." He ordered
limited bombing of North Vietnam and dispatch to South
Vietnam of some ground combat units. In July, after a further
exhaustive canvass of the pros and cons, he authorized sending 125,000 ground troops on the understanding that more
would follow if necessary.

Defending these decisions publicly, administration spokesmen invoked over and over experience prior to World War II.
Rusk was to cite it incessantly. Loyally defending a course of

action which he continued to oppose, George Ball employed much the same brief. He said, for example:

> We have . . . come to realize from the experience of the past years that aggression must be dealt with wherever it occurs and no matter what mask it may wear. . . . In the 1930's Manchuria seemed a long way away. . . . Ethiopia seemed a long way away. The rearmament of the Rhineland was regarded as regrettable but not worth a shooting war. Yet after that came Austria, and after Austria, Czechoslovakia. Then Poland. Then the Second World War.
>
> The central issue we face in South Viet-Nam . . . is whether a small state on the periphery of Communist power should be permitted to maintain its freedom. And that is an issue of vital importance to small states everywhere.[56]

Intra-governmental memoranda may have failed to refer to events of the 1930's because their authors so took for granted the consensus about its lessons that they thought it unnecessary to mention them. Or it may be that these events lacked saliency for many. The Bundy brothers, McNamara, and McNaughton had all been in college or graduate school until at least the outbreak of the Second World War. Rusk, though several years older, had been a professor and dean on the West Coast prior to going on active service with the army in 1940. While all of them had been interested observers (and partisans of American intervention), none had been in public life. It is perhaps not surprising that events after World War II should have been more vivid in most of their minds, and it is worth noting that McNamara, who had been preoccupied with his business career prior to 1961, seldom referred to any event of earlier date.

The "lessons" of the 1930's may nevertheless have weighed heavily with the President's advisers. Certainly they had a place in Johnson's own thought. Fifty-seven in 1965, he had worked in Washington throughout the New Deal years, been

elected to Congress in 1936, and served continuously thereafter
in either the House or Senate. In his memoirs, he says that he
continually bore in mind the failures of the American government prior to World War II.[57] As a supporter of Greek-Turkish
aid, NATO, and the intervention in Korea, he had cited the
teachings of pre-war experience. And his speeches justifying
the decisions of 1965 were filled with similar rhetoric. For
example, he was to say at a press conference that defeat in
South Vietnam "would encourage and spur on those who seek
to conquer all free nations within their reach. . . . This is
the clearest lesson of our time. From Munich until today we
have learned that to yield to aggression brings only greater
threats." [58] Lacking any other record of his private thoughts
during 1964–65, we cannot estimate whether certainty about
the lessons of the 1930's had as powerful an influence on
Johnson as on Truman in 1950. His memoir account of the
critical Vietnam decisions refers primarily to the Korean precedent.

In any case, it is quite clear that beliefs about at least the
very recent past penetrated the thinking of men who determined America's course of action in Vietnam. In 1961 the
examples of France's defeat and of American public controversy over the Korean War prompted doubts. Perceiving South
Vietnam as more analogous to the Philippines and Malaya
than to Korea, officials saw reason, however, to expect that the
country could be saved without wholesale engagement of
American forces. Recollection of the bitter public debate over
the fall of China deterred them from considering seriously
the abandonment of South Vietnam. And the presumed experts on long-term trends encouraged a commitment to South
Vietnam by portraying the conflict there as a planned phase
in a communist timetable for world conquest.

When the Johnson administration faced the choice of
whether or not to go to war in 1964–65, the French parallel
and the Korean War experience still figured in the arguments

against military action. On the other hand, officials saw in the intervention in Korea and other events of 1947–50 compelling precedents for a determined resort to force. Memories of the aftermath of communist victory in China continued to urge them in the same direction. So perhaps did shared assumptions about lessons taught by the experience of the 1930's.

As with decisions by Roosevelt and Truman, so with those of Kennedy and Johnson one can plausibly argue that the outcome would have been the same even if inferences from history had played no part in the reasoning. The Presidents of the 1960's and their advisers saw Southeast Asia as important in itself. Both McNamara and the Joint Chiefs insisted that a position there was indispensable to retention of any defense line in the western Pacific.[59] Kennedy, Johnson, and their associates judged that as Vietnam went so would go the entire region, and they believed that in the Cold War communist success in Southeast Asia would represent an enormous gain to the enemy. On these assumptions, they might have decided to fight for South Vietnam even if nothing in previous experience seemed either relevant or comparable. The only element in the debate that would almost certainly have been different would have been the argument about the domestic consequences of the "loss" of Vietnam, for without recollections of the controversy over China, officials would surely have seen an adverse public reaction as at least no more likely than an adverse reaction to war.

Since arguments from history did play a part in the debate, it is nevertheless apropos to examine here their character and quality. One cannot say, as of the possibly unique case of intervention in Korea in 1950, that they were allowed to preclude other analyses of the issues. Nor, in fact, can Kennedy and Johnson be accused, like Truman in 1950, of over-hasty decision-making. On the contrary, both Presidents permitted months of careful staff work and assigned to it some of the ablest minds around them. But it can be said that the his-

torical reasoning entering into decisions about Vietnam was
at best superficial.

As a rule, examples were cited as if there could be no
dispute about the facts or their meaning, and they were employed indiscriminately in two quite different ways. Sometimes, the surrounding grammar suggested that the logic ran,
"X happened before and therefore X is likely to happen again."
At other times, the implicit logic ran, "Such and such is a
regular pattern in human affairs; X serves as an illustration."
Most references to the French were of the first variety. That
is, the official asserted that the French had been defeated and
therefore the Americans were also likely to be defeated. On
occasion, however, such references took the second form. A
cautionary cable from Maxwell Taylor in February 1965 said,
for example, "White-faced soldier armed, equipped and trained
as he is not suitable guerrilla fighter for Asian forests and
jungles. French tried to adapt their forces to this mission and
failed; I doubt that U.S. forces could do much better." [60]
References to the Philippines and Malaya in 1961 implied that,
since the insurgents had been defeated there, they would be
defeated in Vietnam. By 1964–65, these examples along with
that of Greece had become mere illustrations of the proposition that guerrillas could be defeated. On the other hand,
statements about Korea and about aid to Greece and the defense of Berlin seemed almost always to assert simply that the
past pattern would or should reproduce itself. The same was
true of allusions to the domestic debate over China.

Few of the surviving documents evidence any effort to assess
the actual comparability of apparent precedents or to extend
the search for possibly comparable cases. The only contrary
examples are the Joint Chiefs' comments on the Malayan
parallel and George Ball's evaluation of the Korean analogy.
The chiefs' remark that the French failed to build the Panama
Canal, while effective in debate, hardly ranked as analysis.
Nor did Rostow's memorandum on victory in guerrilla wars.

Even though Rostow had once been a professor of economic history and had written prolifically on the recent past, his memorandum was transparently a brief for a particular course of action and not in any sense an assay of relevant data.

In fact, the historical evidence actually or potentially entering into the deliberation about Vietnam could have received much closer analysis. Where the underlying proposition was that X had occurred and would occur again, the peculiar characteristics of X could certainly have been put under scrutiny. The chiefs' notes on Malaya, and Ball's on Korea, suggest what might have been tried. The chiefs themselves might usefully have been pressed to develop their Panama Canal remark, for it implied that the failure of the French resulted from shortcomings in equipment and technical skill. This contention was at least open to debate.

Where a proposition was of the second type, a systematic review of possible precedents surely should have seemed in order. Thus, for instance, Taylor's assertion about white soldiers in Asian forests and jungles could have been examined in light not only of French experience in the 1950's but also of British and French experience in Asia from the nineteenth century onward and American experience in the so-called Philippine insurrection. In fact, various broad assertions made about guerrilla wars could well have been refined by reflection additionally on some Latin American wars for independence, the short-lived French-supported empire in Mexico, and more recent conflicts in Palestine and during World War II, in Southeastern Europe. Had the war in Vietnam been perceived as in some respects a civil war, attention could conceivably have gone also to sixteenth-century France, seventeenth-century England, the United States in 1861–65, and Spain in the 1930's.

To the extent that the Korean War experience served merely as an illustration of difficulties likely to beset a democratic country waging a limited war, the nature and causes of those difficulties could surely have been better understood not only by a careful review of the actualities of 1951–53 but also by some scrutiny of public reactions to the Indian wars, the Spanish-American War, and the prolonged low-level military operations in Cuba, Nicaragua, the Dominican Republic, and Haiti between 1906 and 1934. Consideration of, say, British domestic reactions to the Egyptian campaigns, the Boer War, and the Palestine conflict and French domestic reactions to the Mexican adventure and the Tonkin expedition could also have been illuminating.

Like the strategic and diplomatic arguments, the historical arguments in favor of war concerned for the most part probable effects outside the United States and indeed outside Vietnam. The logic in references to Greece, Berlin, and Korea ran roughly as follows. Other governments saw in these precedents evidence that the United States would not hesitate to use its military power if an ally or ward were threatened or if an independent state were the victim of aggression. If the American government failed to act unhesitatingly in Vietnam, these governments would infer that the United States had changed its resolve. Non-communist states would doubt American determination to protect them. The communist powers would be inclined to take greater risks in order to gain new territory.

Underpinning such reasoning was a set of unspoken assumptions. In his brilliant book, *Essence of Decision,* Graham T. Allison has pointed out that when thinking of international relations, most of us visualize nations as rational unitary actors, defining objectives, laying plans, and following sequences of coherent actions in pursuit of their ends.[61] In doing so, we ignore important ways in which complex organizations do not behave like individual men and women. We also slight the parochialism, internal conflict, and rivalry which are characteristics of all governments. The authors of memoranda about Vietnam plainly thought of other nations as rational unitary actors. To some extent, they conceived of the United States in the same way, for it was certainly a rational unitary actor that would show determination, keep its commitments, etc. In certain respects, however, they envisioned rational calculation in other governments as different from that in the United States.

Officials assumed that other nations would revise their estimates of the United States as soon as in any one instance the American government showed itself unwilling to wage war. They themselves, however, were quite hesitant to make comparable recalculations even on the basis of repeated actions by other states. They believed, for example, that the United States had faced down the Soviet Union in successive crises over Berlin and over the emplacement of offensive missiles in Cuba. When considering the possibility of mining or blockading North Vietnamese harbors, they recognized that the result could be a crisis with Moscow, for many of the ships carrying supplies to North Vietnam were Russian. Yet they did not read recent experience as indicating that the Soviets would be weak or accommodating. On the contrary, they assumed throughout that the Soviet government had a greater interest in North Vietnam than it had had in either Berlin or Cuba and that mine-laying or the imposition of a blockade would be likely to provoke a war.[62] Similarly, they recalled the crises of the 1950's over Quemoy and Matsu and the Chinese-Indian border war of 1962 as instances in which China had buckled before the menace of American air and nuclear power. Yet memoranda on Vietnam expressed just as much concern about China's initiating hostilities in Vietnam as if these episodes had never occurred. In other words, American officials visualized their principal adversaries as nations whose behavior could not be predicted by individual past actions but which would instead be a function of interests and capabilities.

Had American officials analyzed their own reasoning and,

insofar as historical evidence permitted, that of men in other governments, they might have qualified their forecasts of what would happen if the United States deserted South Vietnam. Their memoranda might have conceded that men in Moscow, Peking, Tokyo, Bonn, London, and even Bangkok were no more likely to revise their expectations of future American behavior than to assume that the action was not indicative of how the United States might act in other situations where its interests were clearer or the odds of success were better.

Finally, to make the most obvious point of all, members of the Kennedy and Johnson administrations could profitably have sought some understanding of the history of Vietnam itself. To be sure, most works on Vietnam were by men who did not know Vietnamese, wrote from French sources, and focused heavily on the colonialists rather than the colonials. Even so, there were books and articles outlining the peculiar evolution of the country.[63] By reading them, men making decisions about Vietnam might have discovered at the outset some truths later painfully learned. Presidents, cabinet officers, ambassadors, and bureaucrats were to speak, for example, of alliance or a partnership with South Vietnam. Any study of the history of Vietnam or, indeed, of the Chinese culture area would have brought awareness that the concept of co-operation between governments was alien to Vietnamese thought. In their tradition, there were only patrons and clients, each exploiting the other. Such study might also have suggested that the separateness of the two Vietnams was largely a Western juridical fiction, not a notion internalized by Vietnamese on either side of the artificial boundary. As indicated earlier, it might also have led to recognition that the conflict in Vietnam was in many if not most respects a civil war, the determining forces of which were outgrowths of the Vietnamese past and likely to be affected only marginally by foreigners.

Given the assumptions generally shared by Americans in the 1960's, it seems probable that any collection of men or women would have decided as did members of the Kennedy and Johnson administrations. Nevertheless, at the moment I write, almost everyone regards those decisions as mistaken. Many find them incredible. It may well be that the fashion will change and that some future generations will see these decisions as not only understandable but also as, in the circumstances, right. I doubt it. My expectation is that, like the decisions of Napoleon III concerning Mexico, they will have a sustained reputation as misbegotten blunders.

Because of this reputation, an autopsy of these decisions provides especially convincing evidence of how history can be misused in efforts to determine the national interest and what to do in its behalf. Here one can see men who would have been scandalized by an inelegant economic model or a poorly prepared legal brief making significant use of historical parallels, analogies, and trends with utter disregard for expertise or even the inherent logic of their assertions. No example illustrates better both the importance of history for men in government and the carelessness and lack of system with which they characteristically use it.

TWO

How the Past Might Be Used

V

Analysis:
Bombing for Peace

Having criticized American officials for using history poorly,
I must now undertake the more difficult and hazardous task
of suggesting ways in which they might do better. This chapter attempts to illustrate how the kind of historical thinking
that enters into governmental decisions might become a bit
more comprehensive and systematic.

Taking as its point of departure the debate of the mid-
1960's over whether or not to bomb North Vietnam, it reviews
a number of analogies that might have seemed relevant to that
particular policy issue. It examines several cases in which
bombing had as one objective persuading another government to come to terms. It asks what study of those cases
might have contributed to the assessment of American options.

To influence decisions in Hanoi was, of course, only one aim
of the bombing campaign debated in 1964 and actually
adopted in 1965. The chiefs of staff consistently argued for
destroying North Vietnam's "will and capabilities," stressing
that, no matter what the political effects, bombing would
cripple the North Vietnamese. Minimizing any prospective results, McNaughton emphasized the symbolic importance of

America's proving itself the "good doctor." McNamara and presidential assistant McGeorge Bundy attached first importance to heartening the South Vietnamese. After visiting Saigon, they wrote to President Johnson: "Action against the North is usually urged as a means of affecting the will of Hanoi. . . . We consider this an important but longer-range purpose. The immediate and critical targets are in the South —in the minds of the South Vietnamese." [1]

Nevertheless, as McNamara and Bundy indicated, weight attached to belief that North Vietnam would bend or change course. Of the principal sub-cabinet officers assessing American options, one of the anonymous authors of *The Pentagon Papers* writes, "the prospect of greater pressures to come was at least as important as any damage actually inflicted, since the real target was the *will* of the North Vietnamese government." [2] And as the other hoped-for results materialized only in part or not at all, this objective became more and more important. Two years after the bombing commenced, McNamara explained to the Senate Appropriations Committee that the United States sought to preserve the independence of South Vietnam and give its people "freedom to choose their own political and economic institutions" and that

> To achieve that goal we must persuade the North Vietnamese to terminate the attacks which they are supporting on those political and economic institutions.
> We propose to do that by proving they can't win their military campaign in the south, and to dissuade them from persisting by making them pay a price in terms of our bombing of the north. [3]

Within the government and in the press, it was frequently argued that North Vietnam was bound to yield when it reached some "pain level." The underlying logic envisioned its government as an individual which would respond to torture as might any human.

During the year-long deliberations of 1964–65, officials did not probe deeply enough into this logic. To be sure, they were warned by intelligence agencies not to count too heavily on Hanoi's changing course, but even the most pessimistic intelligence estimates conceded some likelihood of success.[4] So far as one can discern from available documents and memoirs, no one inquired what precise effects the bombing would achieve towards altering North Vietnamese policy. Some scrutiny of the past could have assisted such an inquiry.

There were many previous occasions when bombing was employed for political purposes—by Mussolini in Ethiopia, the Nationalists in the Spanish Civil War, the Japanese in China, Hitler against Britain, the World War II Allies against the Axis powers, and by the United States in Korea. Most of the time, it had been unproductive. In a few instances, however, bombing contributed to the desired political ends.

In Ethiopia Mussolini tried to compel negotiations through bombing and aerial spraying of mustard gas. He failed. Emperor Haile Selassie continued to resist until every inch of his kingdom had been conquered. In the Spanish Civil War, Franco's Nationalists dropped incendiary bombs on Madrid and staged air attacks against other Republican strongholds, but they were unsuccessful in inducing the Republicans even to negotiate. In China, something like three Japanese bombing raids a day against cities or strategic points in the interior, designed, in the words of the Japanese air staff, "to create terror and excite antiwar sentiments," yielded no Chinese responses to Japanese overtures for a compromise peace.[5] And Hitler's efforts to bring Britain to terms in 1940–41 by bombing shipping in the Channel, blasting airfields and industrial targets, and then, when provoked by R.A.F. counter-attacks, making terror raids on cities, brought forth only defiance from Churchill's government.

The bombing of Germany in World War II is not relevant, for the Allies did not have in view forcing a negotiated peace. Calling for unconditional surrender, Churchill and Roosevelt

summarized the aims of the air war as "destruction and dis-
location of the German military, industrial and economic system, and the undermining of the morale of the German people to the point where their capacity for armed resistance is
fatally weakened." [6] These objectives, it might fairly be said,
were eventually achieved.

In at least two instances, perhaps three, bombing probably
contributed to political settlements. This seems true in the
cases of Italy and Japan in the Second World War, and possibly true concerning the Korean War.[7]

Bombing of Italy began late in 1942, just after landings by
American troops in North Africa. The R.A.F. staged small-
scale raids on northern Italian industrial centers. In the spring
of 1943, R.A.F. and American bombers flew from Africa to
strike docks and transportation facilities in Naples and other
cities of southern Italy. On July 10 the Allies invaded Sicily.
Nine days later, five hundred planes unloaded more than a
thousand tons of bombs on marshalling yards and industrial
targets in the suburbs of Rome.

Causing factory workers to flee or fail to show up, the first
raids produced a disproportionate decline in war production
and provided Italian officials with clear evidence that the
civilian population did not have its heart in the war. Within
a week after the strike near Rome, King Victor Emmanuel
deserted Mussolini, and the Fascist Grand Council deposed
him. Seven weeks later, a successor government signed articles
of peace. According to the King's closest confidant, General
Paolo Puntoni, it was the bombing which precipitated these
events.[8]

In the case of Japan, heavy Allied bombing commenced in
mid-June 1944. B-29's from Saipan hit cities in central Japan.
Through the winter of 1944–45, these attacks centered on aircraft plants. The damage done was relatively small. In late
February 1945 emphasis shifted to incendiary raids on Japanese cities. Nagoya and Kobe were hit. Then, on March 8

a force of 334 bombers struck Tokyo. The resultant fire destroyed one-fourth of the city, killed nearly 84,000 people, and injured 40,000 more. It was the deadliest air raid of the war. Further raids followed, culminating with the nuclear bombing of Hiroshima and Nagasaki.

When bombing commenced, Japan was still ruled by the cabinet which had ordered the Pearl Harbor attack, headed by General Tojo Hideki. A month later Tojo fell, his place being taken jointly by General Koiso Kuniaki and Admiral Yonai Mitsumasa. Following the fire bombing of Tokyo in the spring, the foreign minister of the Koiso-Yonai cabinet approached the Swedish government about possible mediation. In a matter of weeks, Admiral Suzuki Kantaro formed a new cabinet. He said later that he had taken office understanding that the Emperor desired peace, partly because of his concern about bombing.[9] Subsequently, Russia declared war, and Hiroshima and Nagasaki were devastated. Although in retrospect, the use of nuclear weapons makes these attacks seem different from others by orders of magnitude, the actual damage and loss of life did not equal that in the previous assault on Tokyo, and Japanese officials at first interpreted the news as merely indicating that the Allies had developed immensely more effective ordnance. The Suzuki government was, however, alarmed by false warnings from a captive American pilot that Tokyo would be the next atomic target and evidence that the home islands might soon afterward be invaded, and Suzuki announced unequivocally that Japan was prepared to surrender. To this political result, as to that in Italy, bombing made a contribution.

In Korea after the Chinese intervention, an initial rout of the United Nations forces, and the stabilization of a new battle line near the thirty-eighth parallel, truce talks commenced. These talks, however, led nowhere, and a thirty-day ceasefire late in 1951, instead of proving a prelude to a permanent truce, merely saw the communists bring in reinforcements, deepen

their defenses, and at its end, step up the level of fighting.
In frustration, President Truman ordered punitive bombing
raids. In June 1952 American planes struck four key hydro-
electric plants south of the Yalu River. In the autumn of 1952
the President authorized other raids. During January 1953 a
region on the main route between the Chinese border and the
front was bombed continuously for eleven days. After Eisenhower succeeded to office, devastating attacks destroyed six of
the major dams providing irrigation water for North Korea's
agriculture. Meanwhile, the Chinese were given to understand
that if no truce were signed, nuclear attacks might be made
on industrial centers in mainland China. Not long afterward,
the diplomatic deadlock broke, and an armistice came into
effect. Though the evidence is not so good as for Italy and
Japan, it permits a surmise that bombing once again served a
political purpose.

What stands out in all these cases is the fact that bombing
worked relatively little change in the positions or attitudes
of individuals. Haile Selassie, the Spanish Republicans, Chiang,
and Churchill became, if anything, more resolute. While
Mussolini may have been shaken by Allied air raids, he gave
no sign of an altered outlook. Dismissing reports of declining
civilian morale, he told his ministers, "If a war is successful
it is popular; otherwise it is not. . . . We must not be influenced by psychological oscillations. . . . The masses of the
people must be disciplined, that is all that matters." [10] Rescued
from his captors after the coup, he went to northern Italy and
until his gruesome death in 1945 headed a puppet regime
loyal to the German alliance. In Japan, Tojo continued to
argue against negotiations. Consulted by the Emperor in 1945,
he declared, "With determination, we can win!" [11] Had Mussolini and Tojo retained power, the chances are that bombing
would have had no effect on their policies.

In the instances in which bombing probably produced a
political effect, there occurred changes of government. To be

sure, Victor Emmanuel and Hirohito remained, and Kim Il-sung continued as dictator of North Korea, but the two monarchs were more symbolic than actual rulers, and the center of decision in the Korean War did not lie in Pyongyang, but in Moscow, where Malenkov and Khrushchev had succeeded Stalin, and Washington, where Eisenhower had taken the place of Truman. What was crucial in each case was not changes of heart but the fact that events brought into power men not committed to the earlier course of action. In the 1960's it would perhaps have profited American officials to look more closely at how bombing in the past had influenced governmental changes and then ask whether it was likely to produce comparable changes in North Vietnam.

In Italy, the bombing came at a time when many people in government already felt uncertainty about their own futures. Theretofore, factionalism had made Mussolini stronger rather than weaker. His son-in-law, Foreign Minister Galeazzo Ciano, seemed the heir apparent and, as such, had a following in the party. Because of Ciano's youth and lack of gravity, veteran party leader Dino Grandi had hopes either of being himself Mussolini's successor or, failing that, a Richelieu to Ciano's Louis XIII. He, too, had a following. Against both Ciano and Grandi stood various groups, among them one ideologically pro-Nazi and others made up more or less exclusively of military officers or police officials. So long as Mussolini did not commit himself outright to Ciano's succession, Ciano and his friends had to keep earning claim to his favor. Others worked all the harder to edge past the favorite. Rivalries between and within the services, between the army and the Fascist militia and the secret police, all contributed to giving the Duce undisputed control.

In 1942, however, this factionalism became a threat to the regime. At the very moment when the war turned for the worse, Mussolini fell seriously ill. In combination, these developments disturbed Italian politics as an underwater tremor

disturbs the surface of the sea, for Italian functionaries suddenly faced the question of what defeat might bring and
at the same time the question of what might result if Mussolini died.

A host of Italian politicians and bureaucrats took thought
about how they might protect themselves if the worst should
happen. Ciano recorded in his diary hearing high officials
say that prospects were grim, implying that they were not at
fault and that, if only the war policy were to change, they
would do much better. Among these were the Ministers of
Agriculture, Corporations, and Finance, the Under Secretary
of Defense for War Production, the Director of Civilian Mobilization, and bureaucrats in charge of aircraft production.[12]

At the same time, members of two other groups adopted a
parallel line. One consisted of men conversant with the realities of Italy's situation—those whose profession was the evaluation of information about foreign countries. It included
diplomats in Berlin and Istanbul and the chief of military
intelligence. The second group consisted of officials whose
business was internal security—the chief of police, the head
of the Fascist militia, the Under Secretary of War, the commander of army forces in Italy proper, and certain local
officials, particularly prefects who feared that their cities would
become bombing targets.

During the worst part of Mussolini's illness, factions grouped
for a succession struggle. On one side were those whose only
hope of retaining power lay in preserving the German alliance
and continuing the war—the doctrinaire pro-Nazis, the army
chief of staff, Ugo Cavallero, and officers in Cavallero's clique.
On the other side were men whose brightest prospects lay
in a reconstituted regime which broke with Germany and
sought a separate peace. It included Ciano, who was notoriously anti-German, Grandi, allies of the two within the party,
civilian diplomats, intelligence officers, commanders of internal security forces, and generals who were critics or rivals

of Cavallero. In concert and on their own, members of this coalition made contact with the King's household, preparing the way for an orderly transfer of power and the opening of clandestine peace discussions.

Mussolini was, of course, aware that intrigues were afoot. As soon as his health permitted, he tried to put his house back in order. He replaced Cavallero, appointed a new chief of police, and reshuffled the civil ministries, making Ciano ambassador to the Vatican and installing new men in the ministries of Foreign Affairs, Finance, Interior, Corporations, Education, and Popular Culture. But he could not stop what had started. Personnel shifts could not reach deeply enough into the bureaucracy to detach the under secretaries, bureau chiefs, staff officers, and party functionaries already involved in the conspiracy.

Plotting continued. The men favoring a separate peace enlisted the new civil ministers and the new chief of police. Having no stake in what had gone before, the new chief of staff made no move to discourage officers who, if successful, would spare the army further disasters. He also feared that bombing, followed perhaps by fighting in Italy itself, might lead to a popular revolt, of which communists would take command. Sharing this fear and concerned about the future of the monarchy, members of the royal household became more active and established contact with retired field marshals Pietro Badoglio and Erico Caviglia, either of whom might in a crisis serve as Italy's Pétain. They also made contact with the non-communist underground.[13] All the while, Ciano and his fellows remained busy, feeling even more than before that their futures depended on the succession question's settlement.

These *combinazioni* were all gathering strength when the bombing of Rome occurred. Mussolini had already agreed to a meeting of the Grand Council. Ciano, Grandi, and their allies prepared well. The bombing of the capital helped to keep their followers in line, and a two-thirds vote against Mussolini resulted. The bombing also, as we have seen, catalyzed a decision by the King. There followed the unseating of the dictator, his replacement by Badoglio and a cabinet of non-party civil servants, and eventually the separate peace.

Conditions in Italy in 1943 may have been unique. The armed forces had experienced a succession of defeats, and the civilian population was dispirited. Everyone could foresee an Allied invasion which, even if checked, would rip up large parts of the peninsula. Coincidentally, the dictator fell ill, thus forcing the thoughts of people in government to the succession issue. It is nevertheless worthwhile to note that when these conditions developed certain officials took initiatives in bringing about a change in leadership such as would yield a change in policy. They fell into five broad categories: ministers and civil servants mainly concerned with domestic affairs; officials whose business was evaluating foreign intelligence and forecasting the future; officials concerned with internal security; military officers who were rivals of those responsible for the prior conduct of the war; and party functionaries hoping somehow to secure their own futures.

In Japan, the men who engineered a policy change belonged to somewhat similar groups. The context, of course, differed. Not a party-governed state, Japan was ruled by an oligarchy in which army officers were dominant but not at any time in uncontested control. Though General Tojo attempted to monopolize as many functions as possible, he remained subject to the deified emperor and never had dictatorial power. Factions hostile to Tojo and always able to reach the emperor's ear subsisted in the navy, the civil ministries, the aristocracy, the political parties, and the intelligentsia. The structure conduced to political change more than did Italy's.

By the spring of 1944, the Japanese who saw the war as hopeless included men who knew the world outside Japan, such as Yoshida Shigeru and Shigemitsu Mamoru, both former ambassadors to Britain; Kase Toshikazu, a senior Foreign Ministry official; and military and naval officers charged with appraising foreign intelligence, such as Colonel Matusutani Makoto of the Army General Staff and Rear Admiral Takagi Sokichi of the Naval Staff. Their ranks also embraced some men in domestic ministries, but we know less about them because most study of the period has centered on diplomats and military and naval officers. We do know, however, that Shigemitsu, who had become Foreign Minister in 1943, was joined in an effort to bring about Tojo's fall by Kishi Shinsuke, the Vice-Minister of Munitions. We also know that Kase had alliances with like-minded senior civil servants in the Ministry of Munitions and the Ministry of Finance.[14]

By 1944 these men were discussing with one another and with trustworthy friends and colleagues the possibility of a negotiated peace. Similar discussion was taking place among aristocrats and politicians who had been foes or rivals of Tojo before the war. Among them were former premiers Konoye Fumimaro and Admiral Yonai. Conservative in bent, these men feared that if the war should be lost, the imperial system might be overthrown.

All those who wanted a new premier and a new policy recognized that the key to change lay in the Imperial Palace. They all cultivated relations with Marquis Kido Koichi, the Emperor's closest adviser. By mid-1944, after the fall of Saipan, Kido became willing to assist in bringing about the desired changes. He testified later that one reason was his awareness of Saipan's nearness to the homeland and the probability that it would be used as a base for bombing raids.[15]

A conspiracy mounted by diplomats, civil ministers, former premiers, and members of the imperial household resulted in July 1944 in Tojo's forced resignation. The new cabinet contained a number of men disposed in favor of early peace. Admiral Yonai himself became Deputy Premier and Minister of the Navy. Shigemitsu not only continued as Foreign Minister but took over the Greater East Asia Ministry which Tojo had created as a means of circumventing the Foreign Ministry. The portfolios of Finance, Welfare, Agriculture and Commerce, and Transport and Communications went to close friends of either Konoye or Kido. Indeed, the only members of the new government clearly committed to continuing the war were Koiso Kuniaki, the Premier, who was an army nominee, and the War Minister and Chief of Staff.

It is an intriguing and not irrelevant question whether any action by the Allies in July 1944 might have enabled the new Japanese ministry to follow the course toward which most of its members were inclined. Certainly the Allies had done nothing to encourage peace overtures. In addition to calling for unconditional surrender, Roosevelt and Churchill had intimated at Cairo that Japan would be stripped of lands she had held for half a century or more, and Allied propaganda spoke of purifying the Japanese nation and trying her leaders as war criminals. It is conceivable that more moderate or more vague declarations from Washington and London might have emboldened Japan's civilian leaders.

On the other hand, it has to be recalled that Japanese ministers traditionally worked for consensus within the cabinet and between the cabinet and the armed services. Also, some of the conservatives in the peace faction were as fearful of provoking the military as of losing the war. Konoye, for example, was apprehensive about a radical, possibly communist-minded clique of younger army officers. The only evident way in which a decision for peace could have been made in July 1944 would have been for the Emperor to intervene, as he was to do in 1945, and it is not clear that any act or gesture by the Allies could at that point have given Hirohito the requisite nerve or will.

The result was that a year passed before the conspirators succeeded. The change in government in April 1945 strengthened them, for though the new premier, Admiral Suzuki, was

not a strong man, he was not a tool of the army. A special
six-man committee set up to consider basic questions concerning the future consisted of the Premier, the Foreign Minister (now Togo Shigenori), Yonai as Navy Minister, the War
Minister, and the army and navy chiefs of staff. The first three
urged an effort to make peace. The other three resisted
but, aware of growing hopelessness within their own staffs,
did not exercise their constitutional prerogative of forcing
dissolution of the government. Finally, after the events of
later July and early August 1945, the Emperor at last intervened to insist on a decision for peace.

Though this decision was long delayed, the groups responsible for it were very like those responsible for the change
in policy in Italy. They were bureaucrats specially well in-
formed about the international scene, concerned with the domestic economy, or with the preservation of internal order;
military officers who could disclaim responsibility for past
decisions; and men in political life who could both escape
blame for a national failure and hope to succeed those on
whom blame could be cast. A change in policy commenced
with the dislodgement from power of those men who had
staked their careers on the course of action that had failed.
The change was completed when the symbolic national leader,
standing above politics, cast his weight into the scales. Actual
bombing and fear of future bombing—perhaps especially fear
of further nuclear bombing—had some effect on these changes.

With regard to Korea, we lack comparable documentation.
Much of what can be said must therefore be speculative.

America's limited bombing in 1952 and 1953 was not followed by changes in the North Korean government comparable
to those in Italy or Japan. On the other hand, the conclusion
of peace brought a purge in Pyongyang, the chief victim of
which was Pak Hon-yong, who had been Deputy Premier and
Foreign Minister at the outset of the war. A South Korean by
origin, Pak had been leader of those South Korean communists

who had taken refuge in the north prior to 1950, and it seems plausible both that he had been an advocate of initiating and continuing the war and that his dismissal and execution, along with nine party leaders associated with him, resulted from an earlier defeat within the ruling party's councils. Possibly, the triumphant factions consisted of officials alarmed about what might happen to the country and their careers if the remaining fourteen irrigation dams were to be destroyed. We do not know.

In any case, the decision on whether or not to sign an armistice was much less one for North Korea than one for China and the Soviet Union. As to whether there was dispute in Peking over Korean war policy, we are ignorant. Certainly the war absorbed resources which domestic economic planners coveted. They had in view ambitious plans for industrialization and collectivization of agriculture and large new programs for public health, education, and social welfare. Less than a year after the Korean truce, a purge in Peking removed Kao Kang, who had been party boss in Manchuria throughout the fighting. Into Kao Kang's place in the hierarchy moved Ch'en Yun, who was a specialist on economic and financial planning.[16] It is conceivable that this purge was the final, visible outcome of a bureaucratic struggle that involved the question of whether or not the war was to continue.

Certainly there was political change in the Soviet Union. On March 5, 1953, Stalin died. Of what had earlier been going on in Soviet high councils, we have only glimmerings. Stalin's fanciful charges of a "doctors' plot" suggested that some kind of struggle was already in progress. We know that a purge of economic planners had been under way since almost the beginning of the Korean War, and Khrushchev was to say later that Stalin intended getting rid of old Bolsheviks, such as Molotov and Mikoyan.[17] Perhaps there were clandestine factions in Moscow that wanted, among other things, to cut losses in Korea. Certainly, two of the men who emerged with greater power after Stalin's death were to become identified with policies of heavier domestic investment—Malenkov as an advocate of enlarged consumer-goods production and Khrushchev of intensive agricultural development. Stalin's death may have produced a shift in the Soviet government involving greater power for a faction interested in peace in Korea.

That such a faction meanwhile assumed power in the United States is unquestionable. The inauguration of Eisenhower in January 1953 brought in men committed to terminating the conflict. Given the extent to which Eisenhower and his party had capitalized not only on American frustration with the war but also on discontent with existing levels of taxation and economic regulation, the change in administration strengthened congressional and bureaucratic forces interested in checking war spending. Senator Taft, who had never shown much enthusiasm for the war, became much more powerful, and the Treasury under George Humphrey became much stronger than it had been under John Snyder.

There is much that we do not know about how peace was made in Korea. Even in regard to the United States, scholars outside the government lack information comparable to that available on Italy and Japan during World War II. Nevertheless, what can be pieced together dovetails with what is known about Italy and Japan.

Had Lyndon Johnson and his advisers studied evidence from the past they would have asked themselves how the United States might influence a change of personnel in Hanoi, one outcome of which would be a North Vietnamese decision to reduce commitments in South Vietnam. More specifically, what contribution could bombing make? On the basis of previous experience, it could have been inferred that the desired decision would come only if, at many levels in the North Vietnamese bureaucracy, pessimism developed about the war in the south. It could also have been inferred that such pessimism would be most likely to develop first, as in Italy and Japan, within the foreign affairs and intelligence bureaucracies, for it would be there that the disparity between North Vietnamese and American resources would be most clearly recognized. The second key group would have been that concerned with North Vietnam's internal security. Though the peasant uprisings of 1956 had been put down and there had been no recurrence, the conditions that produced them had not significantly changed. Such statistics as were available showed North Vietnam still short of land, seed, manure, and rice. Ho Chi Minh's police undoubtedly worried about what might happen among the peasant population if demands of war in the south continued to prevent improvement in the economy's agricultural sector, and concern about the peasants should have been all the greater because in some areas they belonged to ethnic minorities that made up nearly 15 per cent of the country's total population. Nor were the sources of concern all in the countryside, for there were also Catholics in the cities, and North Vietnam's counterpart of the Chinese "hundred flowers" campaign, briefly permitting relative freedom of expression, had revealed alarming discontent among the urban intelligentsia.[18]

A third group that might have been seen as a possible constituency for ministers or party officials interested in changing North Vietnam's policy would consist of bureaucrats concerned with the domestic economy. The war in the south was eating up funds and manpower that might have been devoted to agricultural development, industrialization, communications, hospitals, schools, and cultural programs. Though it did not follow that officials in agencies starved for resources were necessarily opponents of the war, it was probable that such officials thought mostly about domestic programs, the results they could achieve for their country if given more to work with, and perhaps about whether, if they could not accomplish much, they would be able to retain their jobs. It might therefore have been assumed that if there developed in the foreign affairs and internal security bureaucracies a movement for change in policy, a result of which would be to free resources for domestic uses, some officials in domestic agencies might, like those in Italy and Japan, lend support to it.

Following this reasoning, American officials might have asked whether there was any significant probability that bombing would encourage intrigue within the army against Giap, the commanding general; whether a combination of such intrigue with disaffection among civilian bureaucrats would provide a basis for efforts by dissidents in the Politburo to force an issue; and whether the outcome would be a reconstructed North Vietnamese government which would damp down the war in the south. In the absence of evidence indicating that bombing would contribute to such developments, historical precedents would have argued that a bombing campaign aimed at the "will" of North Vietnam was, to say the least, premature.

This is not to say that historical analysis would have suggested an overt decision not to bomb. For in the past political effects had been achieved by a threat of bombing. Forecasters commonly fell into the error of assuming that bombing would produce more serious economic and psychological damage than it did in fact produce. The English were no less surprised than the Germans at how slight the effects of the Blitz were, and the Germans were as astonished as the Allies that the massive raids of 1943 and 1944 caused so little disruption in war production and public order.

In most instances, bureaucrats were more alarmed before bombing occurred than afterward. They visualized the worst. Once it actually occurred, they saw the results more realistically. They could congratulate themselves on having coped with the crisis and survived. Furthermore, they were angered by destruction of property that was in some sense theirs. Having suffered from bombing, they were harder put to argue for action that would cause the bombing to cease, lest the argument seem a cowardly response to the suffering. In Britain and Germany, the mayors of bombed cities became vocal champions of unremitting war. In Italy, prefects from northern cities that had actually been bombed were backers of war to the death, while the prefect of still-to-be-bombed Naples was one of the peace conspirators. On the basis of historical evidence, it would have been reasonable to assume that maintenance of a threat of bombing might contribute to bureaucratic anxiety in North Vietnam and hence enhance in some small degree the chances of governmental change resulting in a change in policy. But to repeat, the historical evidence would not have encouraged actual commencement of bombing.

Obviously, the foregoing exercise involves unorthodox historical work. It analyzes data in such a way as to suggest a prescription. On the other hand, it is not simply a brief for a particular course of action. For it does not pretend to exhaust the considerations that enter into decision. It says nothing about the probable military or economic effects of bombing. It concedes that the cases analyzed are few and different and that the evidence is dubious on many points. A conscientious historian would add further that the technology of the 1960's was vastly different from that of even the 1950's, permitting far more controlled and precise, as well as more devastating, bombing than had ever been possible before. Moreover, the exercise itself could be said to point out criteria for a choice rather than to indicate what the choice ought to be. Had historical evidence been reviewed in 1964–65, American policymakers might have seen more clearly that it was fallacious to regard another government as, in effect, an individual who could be coerced by pain. In considering whether or not to resort to bombing for the purpose of changing North Vietnam's policies, they might have been prompted to search for evidence as to whether there existed groups in North Vietnam capable of assuming power and likely to adopt alternative policies. They might also have reflected on whether such groups, if they did exist, would be strengthened or weakened as a result of American bombing.

VI

Prediction:
U.S. Foreign Policy
in the Next Decade

A fellow historian once asked me what had become of a former colleague. I responded, "He isn't a historian any more; he is now a political scientist." "Good God!" my friend rejoined, "Next he'll be a sociologist!"

The preceding chapter involved comparisons across geography and time. Although a historian can cite respectable precedents for undertaking such comparisons—as, for example, the works of Fustel de Coulanges, Gerhard Ritter, and Crane Brinton—the chapter was perhaps more in the canon of political science than of history. The exercise that follows has some affinity with speculative sociology, for it attempts to suggest how scrutiny of the past may help in forecasting the future. I should therefore reiterate that both chapters merely illustrate types of work that might be pursued in the interest of government. They might be undertaken not only by historians but also by social scientists, lawyers, bureaucrats, or anyone else who studied and thought about how to locate and assess historical data and employ such data for the types of analyses that have to be made in government.

The preceding chapter suggested how, in regard to a specific problem, a search for useful inferences might be conducted among a range of possible analogies. The chapter that follows is intended to illustrate how comparisons of a broader character might be integrated into that guesswork about the future which people in government must necessarily perform.

The question addressed is a broad one: what will American foreign policy look like a decade hence? What will be the trends in courses of action adopted and pursued by the government? In the aftermath of the Vietnamese war, will the United States revert to avoiding entanglements and commitments? Alternatively, will the trauma of Vietnam quickly heal and the United States resume supporting and defending any and all nations in danger of being taken over by communists? Or will the government follow other courses not prefigured in the recent past?

Anyone writing down answers to such questions risks being proved a fool. In 1933, almost any prophet would have said that the United States was committed to avoiding any future entanglement outside its hemisphere. A decade later Americans were waging war from North Africa to New Guinea. Similarly, in 1943, most people saw a future in which the United States played the role it had not played after World War I—co-operating in the peaceful settlement of international disputes and promoting freer trade. Only a minority foresaw anything like the Cold War, and few if any would have predicted alliance pacts such as NATO or large-scale post-war rearmament.

As of 1963, almost no one would have forecast the conditions of 1973. The preceding years had seen Kennedy's narrow victory over Nixon, the new President's call for re-dedication to sacrifice for freedom, urgent efforts to close the "missile gap" and prepare for "flexible response," bargaining at the brink of war over Berlin and the future of Laos, and the crisis over Soviet missiles in Cuba. It then seemed to most Americans not only right but beyond doubt that the United States should and would defend any threatened non-communist states.

Witness that in October 1961, when Kennedy ordered 10,000 military advisers to South Vietnam, hardly a murmur of public objection was heard; that in March 1962, when Secretary of State Dean Rusk declared that the multilateral Southeast Asia Treaty involved a unilateral American commitment to defend Thailand, no Congressman or Senator and no editorial writer in a major newspaper raised an objection; that in May 1962, when Kennedy suddenly sent 5000 troops into Thailand, warning publicly that they would cross the Mekong if the communists continued their offensive in Laos, indices of public opinion registered no criticism; and that, as late as August 1964, when Congress passed the Tonkin Gulf resolution, there were only two dissenting votes in the Senate and none in the House. It would have seemed most improbable that by 1973, public opinion polls, newspaper editorials, and votes on Capitol Hill would all express strong disillusionment, inclination to withdraw from foreign commitments, and skepticism even about the value of military preponderance.

On the other hand, not all decades have been marked by unexpected turns. The posture of the United States in 1913 was not wholly unlike what close observers would have predicted in 1903, nor was 1933 so far from what could have been foreseen in 1923, even in view of the Great Depression; nor was 1963 so different from what most people might have predicted in 1953. One who ventures to prophesy about a decade lying ahead must try to estimate whether it will be characterized by change or by relative continuity.

In the United States, change or continuity in foreign policies has been determined by domestic public opinion and domestic politics, conceived as embracing Congress, the Presidency, and the bureaucracy. Any explanation of American policies in past decades must begin with explanation of change or non-change in public opinion and politics, and any predictions should be based on a number of specific forecasts concerning likely developments among the public and in each of the places where political decisions are fabricated.

Any general estimate of the public must in turn be built upon a number of specific estimates. First, and perhaps most important, is an estimate of the size and make-up of the population particularly interested in foreign affairs. For the "foreign policy public" never includes the whole nation or even the whole electorate. If survey data are to be trusted, it consists of a minority located primarily in cities, relatively well educated, relatively well-off, and relatively more given to reading daily, weekly, and monthly periodicals.[1]

This minority seems to include not more than 15 per cent of the general public. Such has been the finding of public opinion analysts.[2] And this figure, of course, includes large numbers attentive not to foreign affairs as a whole but to one particular problem, as, for example, businessmen with customers or investments only in particular countries or Americans with strong ethnic or religious ties to other parts of the world. At times of fierce debate, as over isolation versus intervention in 1941 or over Vietnam in 1968, the interested public expanded to include large groups concerned less about international relations than about their own draft status or that of their children, taxation, inflation, or more unselfishly, a seeming moral issue so loudly trumpeted that no literate citizen could wholly ignore it. The interested public, however, probably never remained large for more than a brief period.

Even so, the composition of this public can vary. In the first place, it can be made up of relatively fragmented groups or be dominated by a single issue. In 1933 it included some people who cared chiefly about tariffs, trade, and gold; others more interested in Latin America and the new "Good Neighbor policy"; others who focused on Japan, China, and the Manchurian issue; others whose eyes were on Europe; and still others for whom the League of Nations remained in one way or another a preoccupation. These groups overlapped, but not much. Each had its own profile. None was large. By 1940–41, on the other hand, most of the attentive public fixed on one issue: should the United States act against the Axis powers? And this public embraced groups that had earlier paid little heed to foreign affairs—not only men and women who had been too young but also members of religious groups horrified by Nazi pogroms and the Nazi ideology, people with roots in the various countries which Hitler or Mussolini had conquered, and others aroused by years of day-in, day-out reportage on book-burnings, concentration camps, the Gestapo, the Japanese "thought police," and the cruelties of German, Italian, and Japanese conquering forces. This was a very different public from that of a decade earlier.

Change of another order occurred between 1943 and 1953. It was, first of all, a generational change. Up to the end of the 1930's, people scarred by recollections of World War I and the battle over entry into the League of Nations predominated in the public attentive to foreign affairs. By the late 1940's the majority consisted of men and women who remembered instead the crises of the 1930's. In the second place, there occurred an unexpected non-change. Instead of drifting back into concern primarily about domestic issues, many Jews, Roman Catholics, Italian-Americans, Polish-Americans, etc., retained an interest in happenings abroad. Steadily becoming better represented among the relatively well educated, well read, and well off, members of such religious and ethnic groups figured significantly in a foreign policy public which, as it turned out, clutched "no appeasement" as a shibboleth and proved as militant against Stalinism as against Hitlerism.

In the most recent decade, changes in this public have been in part like those of the 1930's and in part like those of the 1940's. With cities growing, literacy rising, and the college-educated proportion of the population multiplying, the pool of people potentially attentive to foreign affairs broadened. School and college instruction on foreign areas and international affairs, together with increases in tourism and business-connected or service-connected foreign travel, stimulated interest within a more random population. Regular reportage on the war in Vietnam, including that of television cameras, coupled with month-in, month-out draft calls, then brought into being a one-issue public larger than and somewhat different from the public of the early '60's. At the same time, a generational change occurred. A majority which remembered the 1930's was gradually diluted by newcomers who harked back only to events of the Cold War.

Anyone now attempting a forecast must try to estimate what the foreign policy public will be a decade hence. Will it have the same make-up that it has today? Will some elements preoccupied with Vietnam lose interest in international affairs once Vietnam recedes into the past? Will new groups become important components of the public? If so, which groups? Will another generational change take place by 1983?

A forecaster cannot concern himself only with the gross attributes of this public. An equally important range of questions concerns its leadership. Survey data confirm the common-sense supposition that most people do not arrive at opinions on issues by independent analysis. Instead, they borrow opinions from people whose judgment they trust. Ordinarily, the shapers of opinion on issues of international relations are a small minority within the minority, composed of government officials, politicians, and businessmen and professional men with some government experience, connections in high places, many entry and exit stamps on their passports, and the habit of reading periodicals such as the *New York Times* and *The Economist*—in short, an "establishment." [3]

The size and composition of the foreign policy public may be in part a function of conditions within this establishment. The late 1940's and early 1950's, for example, could have seen

much more wide-spread public debate and division over en-
tangling alliances, foreign commitments, and the basing of
forces abroad. Very little occurred. A plausible explanation is
that the establishment was more or less of one mind. With
little or no leadership, no significant public opposition could
take form. By contrast, Vietnam divided the establishment.
Senators on the Foreign Relations Committee, former government insiders such as George Ball and Robert Kennedy, cor-
respondents covering Southeast Asia, and scholars such as
Hans Morgenthau and George Kahin led protest within the
establishment. This in turn legitimized opinion leadership by
others who probably could not have commanded a following
against a nearly unanimous establishment.

Part of the necessary guesswork about the foreign policy
public has to do with the establishment. One can assume that
it will continue to consist of current and former insiders who
are well educated, well read, well traveled, and relatively well-
to-do; but this assumption is of little use for prediction. These
characteristics are shared by a million or more Americans,
including ex-Senator William Knowland and Dr. Daniel Ellsberg. In the 1933–43 decade, the proportion of businessmen
and bankers in the establishment probably diminished. The
Depression clouded their reputations. By the end of the decade, lawyers, journalists, and intellectuals, especially European
refugees, formed a relatively large part of the leadership
group. From World War II into the 1960's the establishment
contained an extraordinary number of people with back-
grounds in the military services or the service departments.
Insofar as there was a visible hierarchy, the top places were
occupied by Marshall, other war-time generals, and men who
had worked with Henry Stimson, notably John J. McCloy and
Robert A. Lovett.[4] A significant part of the establishment's
new blood came later from defense-oriented corporations and
research organizations. One result of Vietnam was an erosion
of public confidence in this group comparable to the erosion

of confidence in businessmen following the Depression. One question about the decade 1973–83 is therefore, What will be the make-up of the establishment? On what types of people will the broader foreign policy public rely for leadership? What consensus, if any, will prevail within this group? If there is no consensus, what will be the lines of division? And what will be the consequences if they do divide?

Still other questions concern variables likely to influence the composition of both the foreign policy public and its leadership cadre. Unfortunately for anyone trying to build predictions, historical experience suggests that the most important variable will be events abroad. Changes in the composition of the foreign policy public in 1933–43 were precipitated by internal developments in Italy, Japan, and Germany, the Italo-Ethiopian War, the Spanish Civil War, the Sino-Japanese War, the successive crises of 1938–39 set off by Hitler, and the outbreak and progress of World War II. The changes after 1943 probably could not have occurred in the absence of communist successes in Eastern Europe and Asia, the attempted isolation of Berlin in 1948, and the North Korean attack on South Korea in 1950. The course of the war in Vietnam actuated the changes of the 1960's. Part of a prophet's task is to imagine events that might galvanize or divide an establishment, define issues for the interested public, or pull into that public groups not now actively interested in foreign affairs. Another part of the task is to estimate the probability that such events will occur.

Turning to domestic politics, one should first try to descry probable trends in the legislative branch. While Congressmen and Senators respond to public opinion, most of them listen to their localized constituencies. The foreign policy public in the district or state of a particular legislator may be quite unrepresentative of the whole. Because Congress does most of its work in committee, and influence within committees varies from individual to individual, the Congress as a whole may, in particular areas, be unrepresentative of the nation.

After World War I, when most observers believed that a majority of interested Americans favored American membership in the League of Nations, the Senate Foreign Relations Committee consisted overwhelmingly of men opposed to or skeptical about such a step. During World War II, the committee did not mirror the change that had come over the interested public. It included a disproportionate number of Senators who could be characterized as isolationists. When Roosevelt and others evidenced uncertainty about whether cooperation with England and Russia could continue into the post-war period, they doubtless had in mind not only questions about the future composition of the public but also fear that, as in 1919–20, the Senate might be guided by its own lights. In the 1960's the Foreign Relations Committee became critical of involvement in Vietnam at a time when polls showed broad support within the specially interested public and its leadership corps. On the other hand, the Armed Services committees, dominated by Southerners with conservative constituents and large military installations in their states and districts, remained backers of the war long after the public mood turned around.

Not only does the legislature not necessarily follow trends in voter opinion, it may sometimes resist currents among the public or itself provide leadership. The Senate guided the move away from internationalism after World War I. Fulbright and the Foreign Relations Committee had a powerful role in fostering opposition to the Vietnamese war. One set of questions for a forecaster thus has to do with the make-up and mood of the legislative branch. What are likely to be the dominant committees? Will the Armed Services committees continue, as in the 1950's and 1960's, to have a voice in issues of international relations equal to or greater than that of the

Foreign Relations and Foreign Affairs committees? Will the Senate Finance Committee and the House Ways and Means Committee elect to have more say than in the past regarding international questions that might affect levels of spending, allocations of revenue, and the balance of payments? On the important committees, who will exercise leadership? What will be their prejudices and predispositions?

Bearing on these questions are others having to do with relations between the legislature and the executive. In the past, there have been swings in their relative influence. For decades after the Civil War, power and initiative lay largely with the Congress. From the late 1890's through World War I, the balance went more and more in favor of the President. Although the 1920's did not bring anything like a return to the 1880's, the decade did see the Congress regain some authority. The Depression, World War II, and the Cold War then restored leadership to the executive. These swings can be attributed partly, of course, to public attitudes. After World War I, many people tended to trust Congress rather than the President because they believed Wilson to have abused his power and to have made calamitous mistakes. From the eve of World War II onward, many saw Congress as a culprit for having kept the United States out of the League, improvised the fatuous neutrality laws of the mid-1930's, and resisted Roosevelt's efforts to prepare for the assumption of new international responsibilities.

Although partially a product of public attitudes, the distribution of power between the legislature and the executive has effects in turn on the make-up of the public, its leadership, and the events to which it reacts. Apart from the fact that the population which influences Congress is divided along state and district lines, it appears to be the case that legislators deal with opinion leaders of a particular type. They talk to people who are locally prominent in business or the professions rather than to financiers or industrialists or professional men with nation-wide interests, for the latter deal mostly with the executive branch.[5] This may mean that effective public opinion is somewhat different when the relative influence of Congress is greater. Also, to the extent that Congress seems in the lead, perceptions among the entire interested public may be affected. It is arguable, for example, that the prominence of Congress in the mid-1930's induced many to see the crises in Ethiopia, Spain, and China as posing essentially legal problems, the reactions to which should take form in legislation. Looking ahead, one must therefore project the relative strength of Congress and the executive and attempt to assess the probable consequences.

The Presidency has to be considered apart. Even in the 1920's the executive retained some power to influence the public and control events. At all times since the late nineteenth century, the President has been by far the most important opinion leader. He has had unique access to information. Since World War II, bodies such as the C.I.A. and the National Security Agency have given him resources which neither the Congress, the press, nor any portion of the public could possibly match.

Within broad limits, Presidents have made much or little of an event and thus determined its importance for Congress and the public. It is by no means unimaginable, for example, that Kennedy could have persuaded the country to see the placement of Soviet missiles in Cuba as an occurrence of minor importance. His Secretary of Defense, after all, shrugged off their presence with the remark, "A missile is a missile. It makes no great difference whether you are killed by a missile fired from the Soviet Union or from Cuba." [6] Nor is it unimaginable that President Nixon could have whipped up a greater sense of crisis about the expansion of Soviet naval power in the Mediterranean. Few if any members of the public can successfully challenge the President's judgment about the proportions of events, and the sense of proportion influences the size and to some extent the characteristics of the public prompted to develop an opinion or opinions.

Speculation about the future thus entails speculation about the dispositions and predicaments of Presidents whose identities and mandates are still mysteries. If the equilibrium does tip toward Congress, will Presidents acquiesce, as did Harding and Coolidge, or will they fight? Will their set of mind be like that of Franklin Roosevelt in 1933—so preoccupied with the domestic scene as to want to minimize foreign affairs; or like that of Roosevelt after 1937 or Truman after 1946—convinced that opportunities for domestic reform are negligible and that the only chance for leadership is in international relations? Will they be visionary activists like Theodore Roosevelt and Woodrow Wilson, or will they be more like, say, Herbert Hoover or Dwight Eisenhower? Wrong guesses on any of these counts could invalidate otherwise well-constructed prophecies.

Lastly, one enters the maze of bureaucratic politics. What has been said thus far has minimized dynamic factors, seeming to imply that the past five or six decades can be set side by side and measured against one another. In fact, the United States has undergone changes of such a character as to make its present self quite unlike its earlier self.

One noteworthy change has been the growth of government. The bureaucracy has become a great reservoir of expertise. Individuals and organizations within it have assembled knowledge about foreign areas and the manifold possibilities for American action. Much of this knowledge has not been shared with the public or the Congress. In part because of the limited time that a President can give to any one area or problem, this knowledge has been shared only sparingly with the White House. Understandably, many people in the bureaucracy have developed a conviction that they are better equipped than the public, Congress, or the President to decide what course of action the United States ought to pursue. That conviction has led them to attempt—often successfully—to manipulate both public opinion and congressional and presidential actions.

The bureaucracy has had a hand in shaping perceptions of events. In the immediate aftermath of World War II, officialdom drew public, congressional, and presidential attention to certain events and not to others—specifically, events on the European and Middle Eastern periphery of the Soviet Union rather than those in South Asia, former colonial territories in Southeast Asia, or even East Asia or Latin America. As time passed, the bureaucracy played a crucial role in shaping public, congressional, and presidential thought. As a result, in the 1950's great importance was attached to happenings which in retrospect seem to have had little relevance to the safety or welfare of Americans—for example, the overthrow of the French colonial regime in Indo-China, clashes between communist and Nationalist Chinese over possession of the Quemoy and Matsu islands, border trouble between Syria and Lebanon, anarchy in the former Belgian Congo, and the civil war in Laos. Kennedy's perception of the importance of Soviet missiles in Cuba was in part a function of what the bureaucracy told him. Certainly this was the case with regard to his view and Lyndon Johnson's of Vietnam.

Also, of course, the bureaucracy has had a large role in conducting international relations. Since World War II it has become increasingly less realistic to think of the executive branch as simply following courses of action determined by the President. Often, Presidents have learned about problems too late to do anything except continue what the bureaucracy had commenced or to defend what had already been done.

To the extent that the bureaucracy independently determines policy, public opinion does not; for the public is heard indistinctly inside buildings in Washington and almost not at all in American missions overseas. Public opinion obtains its force from the attention paid to it by Congress and the President, and when Congress and the President are impotent, so is the public. Moreover, the independent strength of the bureaucracy may cut into the relative power of public opinion even when the President is a fully engaged actor, for Presidents sometimes adopt the bureaucrat's view that statesmanship calls for following expert advice rather than taking a course of action that may be popular.

The would-be prophet must thus face up to yet another group of questions. To what extent will the international posture of the United States in the next decade be fixed by the bureaucracy with only minimal regard for public opinion, the Congress, or the President? Even if public opinion and legislative and presidential politics still determine the broad outlines of American policy, to what extent will the perceptions and agenda of other actors be influenced by the ways in which the bureaucracy reports events, creates situations, and frames options?

These are hard questions, and all the harder because it is almost as simplistic to speak of "the bureaucracy" as to speak of "the United States." The bureaucracy is made up of many components, all of which are different and all of which are subject to internal change. The White House, the State Department, the Office of the Secretary of Defense, the military services, the Treasury, and the intelligence agencies all have unique characteristics. Within the State Department, the various geographic bureaus differ from one another, and functional bureaus such as Economic Affairs, Legal Affairs, and Intelligence and Research differ from the geographic bureaus. The offices headed by different assistant secretaries of Defense are often adversaries, and the relations between the Office of the Secretary of Defense and the services sometimes resemble relations among the colonial powers in Africa during the nineteenth century. Nor are agencies, bureaus, services, and service arms the only units which need to be taken into account, for there are also important distinctions to be noticed between career groups (Foreign Service officers versus others in the

State Department, for example) and, above all, between Washington and the missions abroad, for the interests and perspectives of, say, an army colonel working on military assistance programs in the Pentagon and a West Point classmate heading a military aid mission can be completely divergent.

Just as with the whole polity, so with the bureaucracy the forecaster must begin by disaggregating, that is, by separating large questions about a composite entity into smaller questions about the parts of which it is composed.

First, one ought to ask what will be the distribution of influence among the major departments and agencies. In the 1930's those concerned with domestic affairs had greater stature than those occupied with foreign affairs or defense. After World War II the reverse was true. Presidential priorities provide part of the explanation. Also, however, the pre-war crises and the war attracted first-rate talent to organizations concerned with foreign affairs and defense. Increasing in size and taking on new functions, these organizations offered ambitious men and women opportunities for responsibility and advancement. Domestic agencies by contrast seemed to have had their day, to be custodians of old programs rather than innovators, and to be crowded at the top. One question about the future is whether these trends are in the process of reversal. Will domestic affairs command a larger share of presidential, congressional, and public attention? Will appointive officials and bureaucrats in domestic areas be able to hold their own, or more than hold their own, against people who attach priority to foreign and defense problems?

In the foreign and defense areas themselves, what will be the distribution of influence? From World War II through the mid-1960's, the military establishment was usually stronger than the diplomatic, aid, or information establishments or the intelligence apparatus. Its staff work was better, even on essentially political problems; its recommendations to the President were clearer; and its presentations to Congress and public bodies were far more effective.[7] If the war in Vietnam has altered the public view of the military, has it reduced or will it reduce the stature of the military establishment within the government? *The Pentagon Papers* and other evidence suggest that the State Department showed more wisdom than the Pentagon—and the C.I.A. more wisdom than either. Will the future see State or the C.I.A. acquire the commanding position that the Defense Department occupied in the early 1960's?

An inescapable related question has to do with the Executive Office and the White House. Nixon shifted some functions once thought to be departmental to the National Security Council staff. This staff assembled information, offered assessments of events, and analyzed options for action. The effect of its operation was to reduce markedly the power and influence of all departments and agencies. Speculating about the future, one has to ask whether, if this does not turn out to be a temporary phenomenon, a large and complex National Security Council staff is not destined to develop interests of its own and internal conflicts comparable to those of the State Department or the C.I.A. If so, what forms will its divisions take?

A second major question has to do with relations between the whole Washington bureaucracy and missions abroad. Will the missions be constantly working as in the 1950's and 1960's to induce Washington to attach greater importance to the countries in which they are located? Or will they shift in some degree toward the pre-World War II practice of minimizing the extent of American interest in local events? Within missions, will the balances shift? That is, will military representatives and C.I.A. station chiefs become less or more influential? Will aid and information officers gain a larger voice or cease to be heard altogether? Will all missions follow a single trend; will those in one geographic region differ from those in another; or will there be no pattern at all?

Third, what will be the balances within major Washington

agencies? In the immediate post-World War II period it was by no means insignificant that the best-manned and most energetically led bureau in State was that which dealt with the Near East and South Asia, for Loy Henderson and his adjutants played key roles in pulling presidential, congressional, and public attention to Iran, Greece, and Turkey and in framing the Truman Doctrine. What will be the situation in the State Department in the decade ahead?

In the Pentagon, what relationships will obtain within and between the Office of the Secretary of Defense, the Joint Chiefs of Staff, and the commands overseas? In the first Eisenhower administration, the combination of a weak Secretary of Defense and a strong Joint Chiefs chairman (Admiral Arthur Radford) played some part in making Indo-China and the Formosa Straits cynosures. In the second Eisenhower administration, weakness or uncertainty in both the Office of the Secretary of Defense and the Joint Chiefs of Staff organization made it possible for a strong and confident NATO commander (General Lauris Norstad) to force to the top of the nation's foreign policy agenda the question of whether there should be a multilateral nuclear force in Europe.[8] The balances in the Defense establishment and the personalities of men in critical posts can have effects in the decade ahead.

So can the balances among services and service arms. In the years immediately after World War II, the air force engaged in a campaign not only to establish its independence but also to win acceptance of the twin propositions that air power would be decisive in a future war and that because bombers could not be built overnight, the nation should spend money to keep bomber forces in being. With these interests, the air force naturally joined in the effort to persuade the President, Congress, and the public that the Soviet Union constituted a real and present menace to national security. Subsequently, each service so defined the Soviet or Sino-Soviet threat and the options available for meeting it as to maximize their respective claims on shares of the budget. The result was to force issues to the fore having to do with air bases and missile sites abroad; naval bases in Spain, the Mediterranean, and the Pacific; troop strength and contingency planning in Europe; and military assistance for actual or would-be allies. In trying to look ahead, one must ask how the services will interpret their interests and how, as a result, they will seek to influence perceptions of foreign policy problems.

To the extent possible, one should also speculate about other important organizations. Questions similar to those about the State Department should be asked of the Agency for International Development, the United States Information Agency, and, of course, the C.I.A. With regard to the latter, some guesswork is probably also in order regarding the balance of power between intelligence analysts on the one hand and the managers of clandestine operations on the other. With regard to the Treasury Department and perhaps also the Commerce Department, one should try to envision how officials concerned with international affairs will relate to those concerned essentially with domestic affairs. Will the heads of those agencies be persuaded, as was Franklin Roosevelt's Secretary of the Treasury, Henry Morgenthau, Jr., that the health of the American economy is largely dependent on the health of the international economy? Or will they, like most of Morgenthau's successors, see the protection of American trade and payment balances as their primary business?

As has already been implied, one's guesswork must go not only to the distribution of influence among formal organizations but also to tendencies that may manifest themselves within those organizations. The fact that Loy Henderson's bureau was relatively strong in the State Department did not itself dictate that Soviet failure to withdraw from Iran, Yugoslav aid to guerrillas in Greece, and Soviet diplomatic pressure on Turkey would be defined by that bureau as critical situations requiring strong action by the United States. This result was also due in part to the fact that Henderson was a Soviet specialist long committed to the view that communist expansion would be checked only by threats of force. And the impact of Henderson was equally dependent on the fact that most of his associates and superiors in the State Department hierarchy happened to be Foreign Service officers who shared his attitudes. Similarly, the fact that the chairman of the Joint Chiefs was relatively powerful in the early Eisenhower years did not itself determine that the chairman's influence would be used to promote a focus on Southeast Asia and Formosa. This grew in part out of Radford's background as a naval aviator, commander of American forces in the Pacific, and a skeptic about the Europe-first orientation of war-time and post-World War II American strategy. And the fact that Radford did not always prevail—that the United States did not intervene militarily in Indo-China in 1954—traced in part to counter-balancing tendencies within the bureaucracy, especially opposition from the army. Such manifestations within the bureaucracy made it easier, perhaps even made it possible, for press commentators and members of Congress to express reservations about Radford's recommendations and for the President ultimately to decide not to follow his advice.

Inspecting the future, one must therefore frame hypotheses about currents that will run within the complex organizations that make up the government. Will officials in the dominant bureaus and offices continue to see the world much as nearly all of them saw it in the 1950's and 1960's—as a world around which runs a well-defined frontier which the United States must defend against aggressive communist powers? After the later 1950's there gradually developed an opposing school of thought—one hypothesizing the possibility of a *modus vivendi* with the U.S.S.R. and even with China. The growing strength of this school was evidenced by the limited test-ban treaty of 1963, the Strategic Arms Limitation talks, and moves toward normalization of relations between Washington and Peking.

More recently, yet another school has begun to emerge. It has seen the world as divided into areas in many of which the interests of the United States are of a precise and limited character. Predicting the future involves predicting tendencies of thought within the bureaucracy and their interplay with presidential, congressional, and public opinion.

By specifying and comparing the probable causes for change or continuity in past decades, one can identify at least some of the important questions that ought to be addressed by a forecaster. A historian as such has no special competence for answering them. For what it may be worth I nevertheless record my own guesses—in none of which I profess high confidence.

First, what will be tendencies of opinion within the bureaucracy? Here one must bear in mind two facts. The bureaucracy has immense intellectual inertia. In the mid-1960's, twenty years after World War II, most people in the foreign affairs establishment, including Secretary Rusk and many assistant secretaries of State, continued to regard the public and Congress as instinctively isolationist. Although individuals perceived the Chinese-Russian split as early as 1956, at least a dozen years passed before significant numbers stopped characterizing China as an obedient Soviet satellite or speaking in public of a "Sino-Soviet bloc." Rapid changes of opinion occur in bureaucratic organizations only when there is some large-scale change in structure or personnel, as in the State Department in 1944–46. Looking ahead, one should therefore assume that the bureaucracy will continue to think tomorrow what it thought yesterday and that such a forecast will prove wrong only if major shake-ups occur.

Among the military, there seems every reason to expect rough continuity in opinion. Because the submarine fleet has a role in nuclear deterrence, part of the navy will retain a vested interest in having the President and Congress regard Russia and China as no less threatening than in the past. To justify carriers and carrier task forces, other elements in the navy need the planning assumption that American sea and air power may have to be utilized at any moment in any part of the world. Although some changes may be in process, one would expect navy memoranda in 1983 to say substantially what they said in 1973 and what they said in 1963.

Air force officers can also be expected to continue pressing for recognition of an imminent nuclear threat. Many will be engaged in the next several years in a rear-guard action against critics of the air war in Vietnam. Their official line is and will be that the mistake in Vietnam was to escalate air action gradually instead of following air force recommendations to wage a short all-out bombing campaign against North Vietnam. Air force officers are likely to be the most "hawkish" bureaucrats, and, since they have not had the post in the past decade, one of them is almost certain before 1983 to be chairman of the Joint Chiefs.

The army is harder to predict. Although it has been more involved in the Vietnamese war than either the navy or air force, its middle and upper hierarchies contain many officers who regard the war as an unqualified mistake and, moreover, as an event that has seriously injured the service. It remains uncertain whether or not these officers will gain control. If they do, the army will probably take a "never again" posture in the decade ahead. If they do not, army positions will resemble those of the air force.

In making a projection for the State Department bureaucracy, one must bear in mind not only the considerations mentioned earlier but also the fact that the department's traditions, personnel system, and organization all put a premium on service abroad. It is Foreign Service doctrine that the man on the scene is the best judge of what should be done. Hence in speculating about State Department attitudes, one must think primarily of the attitudes apt to obtain among ambassadors, deputy chiefs of missions, political affairs officers, and the like in American establishments abroad.

Among these men and women, inertia is apt to be complete. That is, one can expect the 1983 cable file from any given capital to resemble in most essentials the cable file of 1973. Communications from missions in friendly countries will continue to speak of the vital importance of the country to the United States and to predict dire consequences if the United States does not give stout assurances that it will carry out its commitments and demonstrate through aid or by other means its regard for whatever government is currently in office. Cables from missions in unfriendly countries will call attention to evidence of lack of respect for the United States and possible hostile intentions but also to all indications that some hard bargains might be driven by skillful negotiators. American diplomats have built up a vested interest in the quasi-imperial status of the United States. They will not easily change stance, and the fact that they live so far removed from the realities of presidential and congressional politics and domestic public opinion makes change all the harder.

About the intelligence community, we have less knowledge to begin with. It seems likely, however, that C.I.A. analysts will also continue as in the past. That is, they will prepare reports reinforcing mission judgments about the importance of foreign areas but also calling attention to the complexities of events there and the difficulty of devising courses of action for the United States that have any likelihood of influencing those events for the better. Operators in the agency, on the other hand, will continue to regard the world as one where forces of good and evil are everywhere in combat and will devise and propose "dirty tricks" to abet the forces of good.

For the whole foreign affairs-national security bureaucracy, I forecast, in other words, relatively little change—a "hawkish" military establishment, possibly lacking unanimity, as in the second half of the 1950's, because of noticeable dissent among army officers; a mission-oriented State Department exerting influence in general for maintenance of the status quo; and a somewhat schizophrenic intelligence establishment. If change occurs, it will come slowly. After all, if bureaucratic politics were the only determinant, we would probably have entered the 1970's with a million troops in Vietnam and more on the way. Change that results from change in other factors will probably be visible in bureaucratic attitudes only toward the end of the coming decade.

Relationships among bureaucratic units, on the other hand, are likely to undergo more rapid alteration. In the Pentagon it already seems the case that the Office of the Secretary of Defense has grown weaker. On the assumption that the decade ahead will be one of relatively tight defense budgets, I would predict that the Secretary of Defense will at no time be more than *primus inter pares* in relation to the chiefs of staff. Doubting that any President or Secretary of Defense will want a strong individual as chairman of the Joint Chiefs, I also predict that the individual services will be relatively more independent.

In State the geographical bureaus will probably retain their traditional pecking order, with Europe, East Asia, and the Middle East ranking first, second, and third, and Latin America and Africa pulling up far behind. Nor does there seem any reason to suppose that functional bureaus will gain markedly higher status. On the other hand, one major structural change in State has at least some chance of occurring. The almost total eclipse of the department after the beginning of the Nixon administration brought new awareness of its weakness in capacity for analysis as distinct from reportage. Elliot Richardson as Under Secretary commenced an effort to build a program evaluation staff. At some point such a staff may give the upper echelon of the department the ability not only to compete with the White House staff but also to exercise some real influence over the geographic bureaus and the diplomatic missions. If so, the profile of the State Department could become quite different.

In the C.I.A. some shift in balance away from operators and toward analysts seems likely. For one thing, the winding down of the war in Southeast Asia will probably lead to the pensioning off of some of the agency's more aggressive field agents. For another, the progress of science and technology in developing intelligence-gathering devices will probably make human spies more and more obsolete.

As for the general question of Washington-overseas mission relations, I would predict that, while mission attitudes will not significantly alter, mission influence will dwindle steadily. This trend will be accelerated if, in fact, the top level of the Department of State becomes stronger. But it will occur anyway.

One reason is that it also seems predictable that the White House apparatus will not become weaker in the next ten years. Future Presidents will probably continue to see independence of agency bureaucracies as advantageous. And my guess is that at least a decade will pass before the National Security Council organization becomes so unwieldy and routinized that a President will feel need to create something else —as Nixon felt the need for a Domestic Council to do what had once been done by the Budget Bureau.

A second reason for the forecast about overseas mission-Washington relations is a belief on my part that the coming decade will also see a continued marked rise in the relative power and influence of domestic agencies. Awareness of domestic problems has, of course, grown. New bodies such as the Environmental Protection Agency and even older agencies such as the Department of Health, Education and Welfare have become able to recruit talented people. By contrast the diplomatic and defense establishments have lost top-flight men and women. Of course, the prospects for solving domestic problems may prove so cheerless as to change the picture, but in a 52–48 call, I predict otherwise.

Broadly, I perceive bureaucratic politics as being relatively less important in the decade 1973–83. Although the bureaucracy will not change much, it will be more fragmented. The President will be more independent of it; the national security agencies will have less influence while domestic agencies will have more; and so long as Vietnam remains vivid in memory, Presidents, Congressmen, and the public will be somewhat distrustful of diplomatic and military figures.

Venturing now into presidential politics, I offer a hesitant forecast that the men (or women) who hold the Presidency during the next decade will all adopt positions regarding foreign affairs resembling less those of the Roosevelts, Wilson, Truman, Kennedy, and Johnson than those of Hoover, Eisenhower, and Nixon. Whatever clarions they sound, they will be hesitant about risking war. The memory of Vietnam will make them pessimistic about their ability to have more than marginal influence on events in other lands. They will see their principal opportunities for achieving greatness as in the domestic sphere or, if abroad, in some capacity as a healer, mediator, or promoter of accord.

The legislative branch probably will have slightly more power than in the recent past. In part, however, this will be because Presidents take pains to share with Congress decisions that may be productive of public blame. The Congress cannot in any circumstances regain a role such as it played before World War II. The demands of electioneering have increased too much to leave Congressmen or even Senators time to master a broad range of complex issues. The seniority system, which might provide a remedy, has proved too often to put the wrong men in the wrong place for a long time. And the pressures on Congressmen make it almost impossible for them to use large expert staff organizations even if such could be put together. It thus seems likely that the next decade will see continued dominance by the executive.

Within Congress itself, one can expect an increase in the influence of Representatives and Senators who were "doves" in the Vietnam debate. Although some elders were among them, they were, on the whole, the younger members. They came out ahead in that battle. Unless forthcoming elections go more against the "ins" than have any in recent memory, these erstwhile "doves" will gain greater and greater voice not only within the committees on Foreign Relations and Foreign Affairs but also those on Armed Services, Finance, and Ways and Means. This drift, taken together with the delayed effects of the Supreme Court's reapportionment decision, makes it likely that the decade ahead will see both houses tending toward opposition to dangerous involvement abroad, skepticism about military spending, and emphasis on domestic problems.

Turning finally to public opinion, I should commence by surveying possible events that might have dramatic effects on the shape or character of the public. It should be remarked, however, that a single event is unlikely to produce great impact. In the 1930's American public opinion was not altered by one happening but rather by a whole sequence, commencing in Asia with the Manchurian incident and in Europe with Nazi Germany's unilateral rearmament. Not the *Panay* incident or Munich or the invasion of Poland or even the fall of France could have produced the same results without much having gone before. Only Pearl Harbor could have done so, and Pearl Harbor could not have occurred except in the setting established by the past. Similarly, it took a host of events between 1944 and 1948 to forge an anti-Soviet consensus, and in all probability this consensus could not have taken shape so quickly in the absence of even earlier events such as the Nazi-Soviet pact and the Winter War with Finland. Short of a surprise attack comparable to or worse than Pearl Harbor, a single happening is not likely to transform the character, composition, or tendency of the American foreign policy public.

The central question to be asked therefore concerns apparent tendencies abroad that might significantly affect American opinion. It can be taken as given that existing opinion tends to be isolationist. As long ago as 1969, polls showed three-quarters of the population doubting that the United States should use force even to resist overt communist aggression against Thailand, Japan, or Berlin. Since then, polls have also shown, for the first time since World War II, a majority accepting the view that the United States need not be militarily superior to its possible adversaries.[9] Although the same proportions may not hold for the public among which issues in international relations have high saliency, these survey results are certainly indicative.

One cannot altogether discount the possibility of a reversal. Chains of events influencing public attitudes need not be consecutive. The Manchurian incident re-awakened fear of Japan which had been quiescent for nearly a decade. Should the Soviet Union suddenly take some aggressive action against Yugoslavia, Turkey, Iran, or some other neighbor or overtly violate arms limitation agreements, alarm could quickly revive. Aggressive action by China could have a similar effect. So, for that matter, could moves by the German Federal Republic or Japan, for distrust of the Germans and Japanese has never wholly subsided. And a second or third incident following a first would undoubtedly produce a marked increase in the level of public feeling.

The public experiencing alarm would, however, be somewhat different from that of the 1930's or of the two decades after World War II. The secular trend in America has accelerated, especially among the well-off and well-educated groups from which the foreign policy public comes. Also, ethnic groups such as Italian-Americans and Polish-Americans are a generation farther removed from attachment to their ancestral lands. It seems most unlikely that at any time in the next decade passion rooted in religious convictions or transplanted nationalism would reappear in anything like its earlier form.

The establishment, moreover, will probably consist increasingly of men and women influenced by the anti-war movement of the 1960's. Sudden changes in the scene abroad could, of course, discredit the leaders of this movement and restore the stature of others, as events of the late 1930's discredited the leading isolationists and brought back the advocates of collective security. Even so, the bulk of the establishment can be expected to remain, at the very least, resistant to revival of a non-appeasement doctrine, distrustful of any row-of-dominoes metaphors, and dubious about public support for protracted conflict. While a massive change in public opinion is not inconceivable, it seems improbable.

Guessing at how bureaucratic, presidential, and legislative politics and public opinion will interact with one another, I would predict with highest confidence that there will not in the coming decade be another round of Cold War. I would predict less confidently that there will not in fact be a return to anything like the isolationism of the inter-war years. Instead, the contradictory pulls of the bureaucracy and public opinion, operating on the President and Congress, will produce continued non-violent antagonism with the communist powers, never rising to a higher pitch than, say, at the time of the Soviet march into Czechoslovakia in 1968 but never allowing for more cordiality than, say, at the moment of President Nixon's visit to Moscow in 1972.

The same contradictory forces should lead to a gradual redefinition of American commitments with a view to reducing the risk of involvement in war for any purposes other than defense of Western Europe, Japan, or Israel, but without overt withdrawal from the posture of being chief protector of the international status quo. In other words, I foresee continued development along the lines foreshadowed in President Nixon's address at Guam in July 1969—the maintenance of alliance relationships with a legion of non-communist states; continuation of military and economic aid at ever diminishing levels (at least in relation to U.S. gross national product and total federal expenditures); but progressive transfer to allies of the burden of providing individually and collectively for their own non-nuclear defense. Sadly, I also foresee prolonged temporization in the face of potential issues posed by a growing U.S. economic presence in that large portion of the planet where people feel themselves relatively poor; for sometime in the decade after next or the decade after that, their reactions to that presence will probably produce events bringing on a new period of change in American foreign policy.

VII

Tasks for Historians

People in government who see value in more critical and systematic reasoning from past experience will need help from men and women who have studied history and given some thought to how work by professional historians can best be exploited.

In episodes recounted earlier in this book, an official or staff aide might have significantly influenced policy by eliciting from historians information about or interpretations of the past other than those in currency. An analysis of the economic history of the inter-war years could have pointed out to the negotiators at Bretton Woods unique features of the period after World War I not likely to be reproduced after World War II. Some data about the 1920's could have made clear to the framers of the Acheson-Lilienthal and Baruch plans a dozen factors distinguishing Anglo-American-Japanese negotiations over naval limitations from American-Soviet negotiations over international control of nuclear weapons. Truman and his advisers in 1950 could have been cautioned of the many respects in which the North Korean invasion of South Korea differed from the Italian attack on Ethiopia or the Nazi conquest of Austria and Czechoslovakia. With assistance from scholars steeped in the sources, George Ball could have added counts in which Vietnam in the 1960's was unlike Korea in 1950 and perhaps made his memorandum more persuasive. By calling on historians to analyze the uproar over "loss of China," Kennedy and Johnson could have discovered that many factors in it were unique and not likely to be duplicated.

It is not my contention that historians are specially well qualified as advisers on what to do. Like other humans, some may be and some may not. Arthur Schlesinger, Jr., appears to have been valued by Kennedy, and on occasion his usefulness was related to his background as a history professor. In 1961, for instance, when Kennedy was considering a settlement in Laos involving a coalition government, he was warned that such a government would be taken over by its communist members. Czechoslovakia stood as the prime example. Schlesinger was able to remind the President that this had not always occurred; France and Italy after World War II offered contrary instances, and Latin America provided others. When records of the Johnson administration come to light, they may show that Eric Goldman provided some special services by virtue of his expertness on American history. Although Henry Kissinger was a political scientist, he had done historical research on both Bismarck and Metternich, and it may be that this knowledge and experience contributed to his effectiveness as Nixon's *de facto* foreign minister. On the other hand, the example of Walt Rostow suggests that imprudent advisers are as frequently found among historians as among any other group.

In arguing that history ought to be more carefully used in policy-making, I would not even go so far as to claim that it is an arcanum, like economics or science, requiring a priesthood comparable to the Council of Economic Advisers or the President's Science Advisory Council. I do insist, however, that historians, like accountants or statisticians, have special credentials for dealing with particular data and that history is not likely to be better used in government unless those who advise on or make policy discover how better to use historians.

For one thing, historians ought to be asked to supply perspective on events in foreign countries. What they say may, of course, reflect bias. If asked in 1961 to account for the insurgency in Vietnam, a historian partial to Diem would not have told the same tale as one sympathetic to Ho Chi Minh. If honest craftsmen, however, each would have distinguished guesswork from verifiable fact and taken care that his generalizations fitted all the discoverable evidence. Neither could have left out of account either the hypothesis of civil war or the hypothesis of plotting in Hanoi to overthrow an independent government in Saigon. Through hearing or reading accounts by either or both, new members of the Kennedy administration might have been led to view with more skepticism the bureaucracy's description of South Vietnam as a free nation under assault by communists following a long-prepared timetable.

In fairness, it must be said that there were bureaucrats who could have provided faithful portraits of the war's background. Some analysts in the C.I.A. and State's Bureau of Intelligence and Research had followed Vietnamese affairs for years. When consulted about prospects for either South Vietnamese success or effective American coercion of North Vietnam, they usually expressed pessimism.[1] If asked to elaborate, they might have explained some of the region's complex history. They were not asked. Except for a few journalists such as Bernard Fall, knowledgeable chiefly about French experience, no one attempted to educate high-level officials about what had gone before. Looking back now, one is entitled to feel that this was at least unfortunate.

The moral might be that intelligence analysts should say more about history. But this is not really their function. Moreover, even if originally trained as historians, as many are, they do not practice as such. They cannot speak about the past with the authority of scholars whose whole occupation is study of historical records and whose opinions are close-hewn by constant interchange with colleagues and students similarly occupied. Perhaps officials would not pause to read history, no matter what its source. One reason why intelligence analysts say little about the past is doubtless fear of boring busy men with data that they may deem inessential. But if officials see the need for understanding history, they ought to seek instruction from experts.

People in government should also look to historians for some information about past policies of the United States. Those who come into office from law firms, corporations, or even universities often have to depend on careerists to explain the setting and context of their new business. Sometimes the careerists are capable of doing so; sometimes not. In State and Defense, where senior officers rotate from job to job every few years, few men have deep knowledge of any particular set of problems. In any case, their concerns tend to be immediate, and their efforts to provide perspective are colored, willfully or not, by their convictions about what ought to occur in future.

When Kennedy's appointees moved in, they were not told much about the past of Vietnam itself, but they were given to understand that the Eisenhower administration had made an iron commitment to maintaining a non-communist regime in Saigon. Belief that this was the case probably influenced their judgment. Later, in any event, Secretary McNamara was to cite as an important reason for upholding this commitment, no matter what the price, the alleged fact that ever since 1954 Vietnam had been "a test case of U.S. capacity to help a nation meet a Communist 'war of liberation.'" [2] In reality, the Eisenhower administration had probably moved only gradually to such a stance. Its leaders possibly never regarded their obligations to South Vietnam as unlimited. Since little evidence has come to light, even in *The Pentagon Papers,* one cannot be sure. A career official familiar with the record, George Carver of the C.I.A., was later to urge Johnson, however, to *return* to Eisenhower's policy, and he characterized that policy as limited support for South Vietnam conditioned on Saigon's demonstrating ability to win, primarily with its own resources.[3] Convinced that the American commitment should be clear, the Southeast Asia specialists in the bureaucracy refrained from informing the new men of past ambiguities. It might have been well if some historian had been on hand to ensure that those ambiguities were not forgotten.

Transitory presidential appointees might also profit from having historians tell them something about the government. For they take over institutions with characteristics and routines developed through time. More often than not, they find that these institutions do not produce the results they desire. Frequently they attempt changes, redrawing the boxes and lines on organization charts. These changes rarely work the intended results.

Some knowledge of history could prepare newcomers for the frustrations they are to experience. For example, although people in the State Department are, by common consent, among the best educated, most polished, most articulate, and most intelligent careerists in the government, Presidents and presidential appointees have generally found their performance disappointing. After only two months in office, Truman remarked "that there wasn't much material in the State Department to work with." Kennedy once exclaimed, "The State Department is a bowl of jelly." [4]

Presidents and others react in such a way because they do not understand the State Department's evolution. Three-quarters of a century ago, a small band of men became convinced that the United States should have professional diplomats comparable to those representing European courts. Volunteers, primarily from the social elite, became the nucleus of an American diplomatic service. While this service was growing, the diplomatic and consular correspondence of the Department of State became heavy enough so that the Secretary felt it necessary to delegate to career officials some responsibility for dealing with it. The obvious model was Britain, where the Foreign Office had a career service wholly distinct from the diplomatic service—a body of men, as Zara Steiner writes, "inclined to regard diplomatists as 'amateurs' and 'social butterflies,' unaccustomed to work or to regular hours." [5] America's would-be professional diplomats lobbied, however, for the principle that the State Department should be staffed with diplomats. They prevailed.

Although the precedent did not always hold and the composition of the diplomatic service changed periodically, Foreign Service officers consistently predominated not only in missions abroad but also in the department at home. Reports from and instructions to embassies were thus filtered by men and women who idealized ambassadors, whose own ambitions looked to heading a mission abroad, and whose prospects for promotion depended on the favor of seniors whom they were theoretically supervising. For historical reasons, the State Department became an institution oriented toward serving and supporting the missions rather than the Secretary of State or the President. In fact, its whole incentive system ran against helping people in Washington make clear-cut decisions which might run counter to advice from a mission or tie an ambassador's hands. Were Presidents and their appointees to be instructed about the history of the State Department, they might have more realistic expectations.

Still another service, for which historians have some special qualification, is analysis of words commonly used in governmental discourse. For each word has not only roots and current definitions but also connotations partly traceable to past contexts. Thus, in one of the best-studied examples, "imperialism" had one signification when coined to describe the governmental system of Napoleon III. It acquired another when applied to enlargement of colonial empires, another when generalized by Lenin to refer to all expanding capitalist states, and yet another when borrowed for such phrases as "Nazi imperialism" and "communist imperialism." Now it is a word unlikely to have common meaning for any two people.[6] The same is true of some other terms employed frequently during the Cold War not only in public rhetoric but even in supposedly reflective reports and memoranda—for instance, totalitarianism and appeasement. And it is true even of neutral words such as, to cite but a few, commitment, credibility, coexistence, deterrent, and détente. Historians can at least help in distinguishing the varieties of meaning which mottle words in common use.

As previous chapters have suggested, the most important function for the historian as historian is analysis of those instances which men in government are most likely to see as parallels, analogies, or precedents. Such analysis may not in itself help officials perceive what to do. They might well decide that their general rule was right even if the precise historical example they had in mind was not adequate proof of its validity. At least, however, the challenge to the example would have compelled closer thought about the inherent logic of the rule; and if it ever turned out that the example was the source of the rule rather than a mere illustration, the challenge might prompt fresh thinking.

Conceivably, historians as such might be asked to identify and analyze a range of possible analogies, such as those arrayed in the chapter above on bombing for peace. In preparation for the Paris Peace Conference of 1919, the British government commissioned studies of previous peace conferences. During World War II, had scholars been asked to re-examine Utrecht and Vienna as well as Versailles as possible parallels for the peacemaking to come, they might have worked out the implications of comparing Stalin not with Hitler but with

Peter the Great or Alexander I or Lenin. In 1950, a historian certainly could have made the point that the North Korean invasion, if instigated by the Soviet Union, might bear less resemblance to the Japanese conquest of Manchuria or the Italian attack on Ethiopia than to Russian efforts to gain control of Korea prior to 1905.

Historians as such could even be enlisted for forecasting exercises comparable to that in the preceding chapter. By and large, they disclaim special qualifications for foretelling what will happen. It was Hegel who framed the maxim that we learn from history that we do not learn from history; and Santayana, that those who do not know the past are condemned to repeat it. Both were philosophers who had had no practice in reconstructing the uncertain complexities of the past. Impressed, in H.A.L. Fisher's famous phrase, with the role of the contingent and the unforeseen, professional historians tend to argue that, if history teaches anything, it is how uncertain and unpredictable are the consequences of what men do. And this book illustrates how often statesmen misguess because they expect patterns of the past to repeat themselves. Most historians would agree with Arthur Schlesinger, Jr., that "Santayana's aphorism must be reversed: too often it is those who *can* remember the past who are condemned to repeat it." [7] Yet it may be that historians come closer than most scholars to engaging systematically in prophecy. For they predict backward. They construct hypotheses about the forces that produced change or continuity in some past period. In the process, they may develop some skill at least in identifying questions to be asked by those who look ahead.

Heretofore, few officials have perceived historians as potentially of much utility. Even were many suddenly to do so, however, it does not follow that historians able and ready to help would easily be located.

Historians who might provide background information about

foreign countries and problems are in short supply. When the
United States first became entangled in Vietnam, no American
had studied the history of the country through native sources.
Even now, few scholars are learned in the history of Thailand,
Burma, Malaya, Singapore, Indonesia, or even the Philippines.
Despite government and foundation encouragement of area
studies, the same statement holds true for most countries of
South Asia, the Middle East, Africa, Latin America, and for
that matter, Southern, Southeastern, East Central, and North-
ern Europe.

While more numerous and more ready to deal with very
recent events, historians concerned with American politics or
governmental processes or the kinds of historical instances
that figure in Washington debate know relatively little about
periods and events which seem most relevant to people in
power. At present, the principal historical records of the American government are open only through 1946. It is possible
to write with some confidence about the intervention in Korea
in 1950 only because of the exhaustive congressional investigation of 1951, and about decisions on Vietnam of the 1960's
only because of unauthorized publication of *The Pentagon
Papers*. With regard to most occurrences and developments of
the Cold War, professional historians can discover only what
appears in public texts, periodicals, and newspapers. They
cannot easily therefore help officials to gain perspective on
current policies or institutions or see freshly the half-remembered events which seem to them to convey lessons.

If government is to be better served by the historical profession, there must, in the first place, come into being a larger
corps of scholars expert on the modern history of out-of-the-
way places and regions. Most historians work on the English-
speaking nations or Western Europe. After World War II,
the government and foundations spent a lot of money to encourage study of Russia and China. As a result, a respectable
number of specialists know the history of these countries and

also of Japan. For most other parts of the world, this is not the case. If officials should suddenly need perspective on events in, say, Thailand, Iraq, Rhodesia, Venezuela, Yugoslavia, or Finland, they would be almost as hard put as with regard to Vietnam in the 1960's.

If there are to be historians expert on such countries, they have to develop long before a need for them becomes evident. They have to learn the skills of their discipline, acquire the necessary languages, obtain some first-hand knowledge of geography, customs, and culture, and immerse themselves in the records. This takes years.

Most historians are now bunched in a few fields because they are teachers as well as scholars, and they teach the subjects that are popular among students. This is not only because they like audiences but also because universities necessarily allocate professorships in part on the basis of student interest. Those who have become expert on Russia or China or Japan have done so with the enticement not only of generous training fellowships but also prospects that either student demand or outside funding would ensure opportunities for permanent academic employment. It follows that historians expert on a broader spectrum of countries and areas will emerge only if the government, foundations, and other benefactors of higher education provide support for their training, travel, and research and for endowed or permanently financed chairs in their specialties. While it cannot be argued that there is a plain, immediate national need, it certainly can be contended that contingencies may arise when historical knowledge and understanding could contribute to wise action and that it may make as much sense to spend money preparing for these contingencies as to spend it on exotic weapons research in preparation for the equally uncertain contingencies of war.

Of historians expert on past policies of the United States or American governmental institutions or episodes in past international relations, there is no comparable shortage. Moreover, these scholars show no disinclination to deal with subjects potentially of interest to people in government. Unlike some of their colleagues, they have no tradition of insisting that decades or centuries must pass before events can be treated as history. On the contrary, their custom is to commence research and analysis as soon as any significant body of primary sources becomes available.

What these historians chiefly need is information—access to records, both written and oral, concerning relatively recent events. To some extent, foreign area specialists share the same need. If ever asked for counsel, they should be able to speak with knowledge of all or most of the available evidence. Over the years, they should have stored away in their heads not only the contents of public records but also those of American embassy reports, intelligence summaries, and the like—perhaps not yesterday's, but certainly those of a few years back. As a practical matter, most of these area specialists could probably be accommodated by being appointed, with the necessary clearances, as unpaid consultants to the State Department or the C.I.A. The two or three people in the country specializing in the history of Thailand, for example, could easily be brought into the small circle of desk officers and intelligence analysts who deal with that country in Washington. For historians who need to examine a spectrum of records, to investigate the workings of the American government, and to analyze high-level decisions, no such simple expedient suggests itself.

From the historian's standpoint, it would be ideal to have all records open for free research. Most would concede, however, that this is impractical. Even if security classification of documents is frequently unjustified, the files do contain material which, most people would agree, should remain secret —for example, formulas or designs for nuclear, radiological, biological, or chemical weapons and reports which could compromise the safety of informants in other countries.

The files contain a great deal more material appropriately characterized as sensitive. Some could embarrass individuals or harm their careers, as happened to the State Department's China hands when their candid reports on the corruptness of Chiang's regime came to the notice of pro-Nationalist Congressmen. Some could embarrass whole departments or agencies if misused by journalists or headline-hunting legislators, as on more than one occasion were the documents gathered by Drew Pearson, Jack Anderson, and other sensational columnists and by investigators for the Senate Internal Security Subcommittee and the House Committee on Un-American Activities. Furthermore, much of what is put on paper within the government deserves confidentiality at least for some period, just as do internal communications within business firms or newspaper or magazine offices or political organizations. Otherwise, people in government would always be composing press releases instead of reports or memoranda about problems in hand. Government records thus can be opened for wholesale research only after some lapse of time, and even then provision must be made for keeping exceptional documents locked away for a longer period.

The existing system—if it can be called that—does not answer the needs of either historians or the government. The State Department opens records only after publication of its documentary *Foreign Relations* series. At present, therefore, research is permissible in files more than a quarter-century old. The department's highest hope, uncertain of fulfillment, is to reduce the interval to twenty years. In practice, post-World War II Defense Department records are largely inaccessible. Those of the C.I.A., the code-breaking National Security Agency, and the National Security Council are wholly closed. Indeed, fully cleared official researchers have difficulty getting at them. Historians are handicapped in attempting to analyze most events in living memory, and the government thus denies itself professional assistance in reconstructing and interpreting the very events which most officials are apt to regard as relevant and instructive.

This situation could easily be remedied. President Nixon took a first step in 1972 with an executive order specifying that, as a general rule, even highly classified papers ought to become open after ten years.[8] Unfortunately, the rule admits so many exceptions as to have little probable effect. The exemption, for example, of "material disclosing a system, plan, installation, project or specific foreign relations matter the continuing protection of which is essential to the national security" could cover all documents concerning American relations with any nation except possibly one that had ceased to exist. But legislation or further administrative action or both could actually open up almost all records of more than a certain age. As recently proposed by the American Historical Association, declassification could be automatic for all except narrowly defined categories such as personnel and investigatory files, and any other exceptions could be submitted for final and exclusive judgment to an independent commission.[9]

Even if records were to be substantially opened after ten years, gaps would persist. The archives are so voluminous, the interests of historians are so varied, and the processes of research, writing, and publication are so slow that another half-decade or decade would pass before articles and books appeared in print. The knowledge shared by professional historians, and thus the knowledge available to the government through them, would still leave the last fifteen or twenty years out of account. If the bureaucracy were to insist upon a later cut-off for opening files—say, fifteen or twenty years, the monographic literature would remain even farther behind the present.

This gap could be narrowed, however, if the fixing of a date for the general opening of archives were accompanied by expansion and acceleration of official or officially sponsored historical work.

At present, the State Department's Historical Office engages chiefly in preparing the *Foreign Relations* series and assisting private scholars in use of pre-1946 files. In view of the increasing volume of material, the editors of *Foreign Relations* have already had to become much more selective than when preparing volumes for pre-World War II years. They could become more selective still, publishing significant documents from the administrations just preceding the one currently in office, summarizing where possible the gist of key documents which could not yet be declassified, and otherwise locating and providing finding aids for the material that is to become public at the end of whatever period statute or executive order specifies.

The Office of the Secretary of Defense, the services, the C.I.A., and other agencies could do likewise. Alternatively, their numerous historians could produce and publish monographs like those in the army's superb history of World War II or general histories of the agency's work, like the equally fine volumes which describe the background and early history of the Atomic Energy Commission.

Documentary publications and published official histories could at least ensure that the events most fresh in the minds of people in government were not blank areas for historians from whom they might seek assistance.

Further, some outside historians might be authorized or actually invited to use records not yet generally open. The 1972 presidential executive order envisions granting access to classified data "to persons outside the executive branch who are engaged in historical research projects," provided that access is "clearly consistent with the interests of national security" and that steps are taken to ensure against public disclosure of genuinely secret or sensitive information. Under this or an amended order or corresponding legislation, some committee or board might be able to approve a wide range of research projects, providing only that the researcher agreed, perhaps under pain of criminal penalties, not to disclose or publish his results until either he had official approval or the period arrived when his research materials were automatically declassified.

In some instances, officials actually ought to ask for research —subject, probably, to the same qualifications. Recognizing the danger of ill-informed "revisionism" such as that after World War II, members of Truman's cabinet commissioned William L. Langer and S. Everett Gleason to write a full study of American intervention in World War II. Completed and published early in the 1950's, it had the intended effect. Also, perhaps, its publication had something to do with the otherwise puzzling fact that the destroyer deal and lend-lease seldom figured in the superficial analogies of officials and journalists discussing post-war aid programs. Not all such ventures were equally successful. Hoping to lessen public misunderstanding of the American role in the Chinese revolution, Acheson invited Herbert Feis to write *The China Tangle*. Though of high quality, the book did not achieve its purpose.[10] Nevertheless, for the public's education, or even more for their own, officials might commission comparable studies. Surely members of the Johnson administration would themselves have benefited from having in hand a history of Eisenhower's policies in Southeast Asia, and the successors to President Nixon should want a full account of how he pursued stabilization of relations with China and the Soviet Union.

The Pentagon Papers illustrates how important it is that any such histories be prepared for publication. Although the documents in that study are of enormous value, the text is, on the whole, verbose, superficial, and of considerably less than professional quality. A major reason is that the authors wrote anonymously and with no expectation that their work would be scrutinized by other scholars. If the government is to get good history, it will get it only from historians who know that they will be held to account by their peers for the thoroughness, accuracy, and objectivity of what they write.

Most of the foregoing stresses historians' interests. If everything suggested were to come about, there would be training fellowships, research funds, and professorships for foreign area specialists, freer access by all to research materials, and more publication by the government of documents and other works which historians want for their writing and teaching. Even if government officials accepted fully the argument that some assistance from historians could benefit them, the question remains open whether they would actually get what they wanted and needed or whether what they got would be worth the price.

For what is suggested here is plainly not free of cost. The development and maintenance of historians expert on lesser countries and regions would, of course, take money. Executive agencies, the Office of Management and Budget, and Congress would have to decide that money was better spent for this purpose than for others.

Of still more importance, probably, are potential costs in the peace of mind of people in government. Most of them will concede that the large majority of classified documents do not need or deserve to be kept secret for more than a short period of time. Concerning those of the Department of Defense, a former air force security officer has testified that "the disclosure of information in at least 99½ per cent of those classified documents could not be prejudicial to the defense interests of the nation." [11] Even officials accepting such an estimate could still feel, however, that concealment of the remaining ½ per cent was of such importance as to justify withholding all or most of the remainder.

The sensitivity within the bureaucracy can hardly be overstated. In the State Department, diplomats fear compromising personal relationships with people in other governments. The geographical bureaus have often opposed release of documents twenty or more years old because they contained critical comments about men still alive in other capitals. Further, diplomats assert that officials will not speak candidly or negotiate freely if afraid that what they say or propose may eventually become public. And remembering the China hands of the 1940's, almost every Foreign Service officer worries about attracting attention in the press or Congress.

Military men tend to be even more touchy than diplomats. Officially, the Joint Chiefs of Staff take the position that their documents should not become public because, even if wholly harmless in substance, they might reveal Joint Staff procedures and thus give a potential enemy an advantage in estimating what the United States would or could do in war time. Officials in the C.I.A. similarly worry not only about jeopardizing sources of information and operational plans but about giving a potential enemy clues to how the agency works. Their classification manual is itself a classified document. And the National Security Agency outdoes all others. Access to messages which it intercepts or decodes is limited to a small, specially cleared group, the members of which take an oath not even to discuss these messages with others. On occasion—as, for example, with regard to the Tonkin Gulf incidents—the whole credibility of the government has come into question because even the highest officials dared not mention publicly communications intelligence on which their decisions were based.

The vision of potentially irresponsible scholars rummaging among diplomatic and intelligence cables, military planning papers, and past communication intercepts horrifies people in the bureaucracy. While scholars might wish this were not so, they cannot ignore it as a fact. Of course, executive orders could be issued or legislation passed without regard to bureaucratic sensibilities, but this is not likely to happen. Presidents and Congressmen recognize that the government can no more function without co-operative bureaucrats than a factory can function without co-operative workers. Diplomats, intelligence agents, military officers, and code breakers have to have some sense of security in order to work effectively. Moreover, if they become sufficiently apprehensive of the effects of opening archives or authorizing or commissioning historical studies, they could and would subvert the entire enterprise by ceasing to put things on paper, taking care promptly to destroy documents of any conceivable sensitivity, or otherwise rigging the record. Any efforts to improve the scope and currency of historical studies must be so designed as to reassure the bureaucracy that the ½ per cent or 10 per cent or whatever it is of truly secret or sensitive information will not thereby find its way into the newspapers or the files of foreign intelligence services.

Perhaps even more important are the potential costs in time. To people high in government, nothing is more valuable. They are deluged by paper. On almost any day, they have to set aside some seemingly urgent matters in order to deal with others still more urgent. While many might accept the abstract argument that they should have fuller and more precise historical information, it does not follow that, in practice, they would judge reading or hearing history the most profitable way to employ a marginal hour.

The problem is all the greater because history is not easily condensed. The historian's generalizations explain evidence, and they are seldom meaningful unless at least some of the evidence is presented along with them. Moreover, most historians by training and perhaps temperament tend to err on the side of giving too much detail and introducing too many qualifications. Expressing doubt that historians could in practice be helpful to him, one State Department officer remarked, "Historians refuse to generalize . . . to give up detail and to give up shadings." [12] If history is to be better used in government, nothing is more important than that professional historians discover means of addressing directly, succinctly, and promptly the needs of people who govern.

Having singled out some services that historians might perform, some ways in which they might become better equipped to do so, and some obstacles to their actually being called upon to serve, I obviously ought to conclude with some programmatic recommendations. I shall not do so. The reasonableness of federal support for foreign area studies, freer opening of archives, and an increase in historical studies permitted or sponsored by the government seems to me self-evident. On the other hand, I have too much the perspective of a scholar and the academy to perceive more than superficially the problems visible to budget-framers, Congressmen, bureaucrats, and preoccupied men and women high up in the executive branch.

Earlier chapters attempted to establish the point that history is important to people in government. Men and women making decisions under conditions of high uncertainty necessarily envision the future partly in terms of what they believe to have happened in the past. Their understanding of the present is shaped by what they think to have gone before. Often, their knowledge of what in fact occurred earlier is shallow or faulty, and deficiencies in information breed greater deficiencies in reasoning. Having learned not to trust inexpert guesswork where numbers, economic models, or scientific formulas are concerned, perhaps they will see that they also need clearer understanding of the history that so often imprisons them.

Acknowledgments

In the notes for each chapter I have tried to thank those people who helped me understand or interpret some particular problem. Here, I want to express indebtedness to those from whom I have been learning to think about a spread of issues of which those touched on in this volume form only a subset.

For the past half-dozen years it has been my privilege to take part in what is now the Research Seminar of the Institute of Politics of the John F. Kennedy School of Government at Harvard. Starting with shared puzzlement as to why outcomes in government so seldom resemble what was intended by the people who govern, the Seminar first concentrated on deciphering the interplay between policy-setters and bureaucracies. Over time it has turned its attention more and more to the mental processes of people at all levels in government on the one hand and on the other hand the practical question of how analysis might develop solutions to public policy problems that would not only look right on a blackboard but actually take effect out in the world. In one way or another, all of these interests are reflected in this book.

The work which is most nearly a product of the Research

Seminar is Graham T. Allison, *The Essence of Decision: Explaining the Cuban Missile Crisis* (Boston: Little, Brown, 1971). Other books which bear its marks are Fred C. Iklé, *Every War Must End* (New York: Columbia University Press, 1971); Richard E. Neustadt, *Alliance Politics* (New York: Columbia University Press, 1970); and Samuel R. Williamson, Jr., *The Politics of Grand Strategy: Britain and France Prepare for War, 1904–1914* (Cambridge: Harvard University Press, 1969). The next major work to issue directly from the Seminar will be a study by John D. Steinbruner exploring the abortive multilateral nuclear force proposals of the late 1950's and early 1960's but using that case as a vehicle for examining modes of perception within government. Anyone who reads my pages will see points of filiation with all these works.

I cannot adequately express my intellectual debt to Messrs. Allison, Iklé, Neustadt, Williamson, Steinbruner, and to others who, over the years, have taken part in the Research Seminar, among them Francis M. Bator, Joseph L. Bower, William C. Capron, Michel Crozier, Morton H. Halperin, Philip B. Heymann, Albert O. Hirschman, Stanley Hoffmann, Henry D. Jacoby, William W. Kaufmann, Andrew W. Marshall, Don K. Price, Edwin O. Reischauer, Henry S. Rowen, Thomas C. Schelling, James Q. Wilson, and Adam Yarmolinsky.

Recently, the Research Seminar formed a sub-group concerned specifically with historical studies. I am indebted to its members not only for general wisdom but also for specific comments on early drafts of my first two chapters. Those who are not members of the larger Seminar are Diane Shaver Clemens, Anne Karalekas, Thomas E. Lifka, Charles S. Maier, Martin H. Peretz, Steven L. Rearden, Martin Weil, and Daniel Yergin.

I owe further debts to students who have participated with me in the last few years in graduate seminars and to various people with whom I have had the opportunity to discuss themes appearing in this book, particularly my colleagues,

Robert L. Jervis and James C. Thomson, Jr., my old friend Louis Morton, and the great participant-historian, now deceased, Herbert Feis. To Henry Owen, I have a special obligation, for he took time to read the entire manuscript and provide reactions based on his long experience in government.

Lastly, I must thank Mary Ellen Gianelloni who, with unfailing cheerfulness, converted my seemingly endless revisions into impeccable typescript.

E.R.M.

Notes

Preface

1. Charles Seymour, ed., *The Intimate Papers of Colonel House*, 4 vols. (Boston: Houghton Mifflin, 1926–28), I, pp. 303–4; Ernest R. May, *The World War and American Isolation, 1914–1917* (Cambridge: Harvard University Press, 1959), pp. 54–71.

2. Hans L. Trefousse, *Germany and American Neutrality, 1935–1941* (New York: Bookman Associates, 1951), pp. 35 ff.; Saul Friedländer, *Prelude to Downfall: Hitler and the United States, 1935–1941* (English translation; New York: Alfred A. Knopf, 1967), pp. 56–65; James V. Compton, *The Swastika and the Eagle: Hitler, the United States, and the Origins of World War II* (Boston: Houghton Mifflin, 1967), pp. 148–60.

3. Anthony Eden, *Full Circle* (Boston: Houghton Mifflin, 1960), p. 578.

4. The basic text is Lionel Festinger, *A Theory of Cognitive Dissonance* (Evanston, Ill.: Row, Peterson, 1954).

5. John F. Kennedy, *Profiles in Courage* (New York: Harper, 1956).

6. Robert F. Kennedy, *Thirteen Days: A Memoir of the Cuban Missile Crisis* (New York: W. W. Norton, 1969), p. 40; Arthur M. Schlesinger, Jr., *A Thousand Days: John F. Kennedy in the White House* (Boston: Houghton Mifflin, 1965), pp. 803, 806–7.

I   World War II: Preparing for the Last Peace

A very early version of this chapter was presented to the American Political Science Association in 1966. I am grateful for comments made then by Arthur M. Schlesinger, Jr. and Stephen Kertesz.

In addition to those cited in notes below, works on which the chapter draws heavily are James MacGregor Burns, *Roosevelt: The Soldier of Freedom* (New York: Harcourt Brace Jovanovich, 1970); Robert A. Divine, *Second Chance: The Triumph of Internationalism in America during World War II* (New York: Atheneum, 1967); Herbert Feis, *Churchill, Roosevelt, Stalin: The War They Waged and the Peace They Sought* (Princeton: Princeton University Press, 1957); Willard Range, *Franklin D. Roosevelt's World Order* (Athens: University of Georgia Press, 1959); and Ruth B. Russell, *A History of the United Nations Charter: The Role of the United States, 1940–1945* (Washington, D.C.: The Brookings Institution, 1958).

1. Samuel I. Rosenman, ed., *The Public Papers and Addresses of Franklin D. Roosevelt,* 13 vols. (New York: Harper and Brothers, 1938–50), XII, pp. 553–62.
2. Samuel I. Rosenman, *Working with Roosevelt* (New York: Harper and Brothers, 1952), p. 412; Elting E. Morison, *Turmoil and Tradition: A Study of the Life and Times of Henry L. Stimson* (Boston: Houghton Mifflin, 1960), pp. 594–95; 89 Cong., 1 sess., U.S. Senate, Committee on the Judiciary, Internal Security Subcommittee, *Morgenthau Diary (China),* II, pp. 963ff.
3. *United States News,* XV (Dec. 31, 1943), p. 28.
4. *Ibid.,* XVI (Jan. 14, 1944), p. 6.
5. Hadley Cantril, ed., *Public Opinion 1935–1946* (Princeton: Princeton University Press, 1951), pp. 367, 373, 944.
6. Robert E. Sherwood, *Roosevelt and Hopkins* (New York: Harper and Brothers, 1948), p. 697.
7. 90 Cong., 1 sess., U.S. Senate, Committee on the Judiciary, Internal Security Subcommittee, *Morgenthau Diary (Germany),* p. 443.
8. Harley F. Notter *et al., Postwar Foreign Policy Planning* (Wash-

ington, D.C.: U.S. Department of State, 1949), pp. 387–90, 428–
34; Walter Millis, ed., *The Forrestal Diaries* (New York: Viking
Press, 1951), pp. 8, 33, 37–38.

9. Roy Harrod, *The Dollar* (2nd ed.; New York: W. W. Norton,
1963), pp. 93ff.; Walt W. Rostow, *The United States in the World
Arena* (New York: Harper and Brothers, 1960), p. 133; Richard
N. Gardner, *Sterling—Dollar Diplomacy* (new expanded ed.; New
York: McGraw-Hill, 1969), pp. 5–6.

10. Robert A. Divine, *Roosevelt and World War II* (Baltimore: Johns
Hopkins University Press, 1969), pp. 60–65.

11. *Public Papers of Franklin D. Roosevelt*, XIII, p. 142.

12. *Ibid.*, p. 350.

13. Edward J. Rozek, *Allied Wartime Diplomacy: A Pattern in Poland*
(New York: John Wiley and Sons, 1958), p. 298; Sherwood, *Roosevelt and Hopkins*, p. 870.

14. *Public Papers of Franklin D. Roosevelt*, XIII, p. 32.

15. U.S. Department of State, *Foreign Relations of the United States,
1945: The Conferences at Malta and Yalta*, p. 617.

16. *Ibid., 1943: The Conferences at Cairo and Teheran*, p. 259.

17. Information from Professor Dexter Perkins, who interviewed Halifax during World War II.

II The Cold War: Preventing World War II

This chapter draws on a number of works other than those
cited in notes below, among them: George Curry, *James F.
Byrnes* (New York: Cooper Square Publishers, 1965); Herbert
Feis, *From Trust to Terror: The Onset of the Cold War, 1945–
1950* (New York: W. W. Norton, 1970); Richard M. Freeland,
*The Truman Doctrine and the Origins of McCarthyism: For-
eign Policy, Domestic Politics, and Internal Security, 1946–
1948* (New York: Alfred A. Knopf, 1972); Lloyd C. Gardner,
*Architects of Illusion: Men and Ideas in American Foreign
Policy, 1941–1949* (Chicago: Quadrangle Books, 1972); Ga-
briel Kolko and Joyce Kolko, *The Limits of Power: The World
and United States Foreign Policy, 1945–1954* (New York: Alfred A. Knopf, 1972); W. Averell Harriman, *America and Russia in a Changing World: A Half Century of Personal Observation* (Garden City, N.Y.: Doubleday, 1971); Walter LaFeber,

America, Russia, and the Cold War, 1945–1966 (New York:
John Wiley and Sons, 1967); Charles S. Maier, "Revisionism
and the Interpretation of Cold War Origins," *Perspectives in
American History,* IV (1970), pp. 313–50; and Adam B. Ulam,
The Rivals: America and Russia since World War II (New
York: The Viking Press, 1971).

In addition, I have profited immensely from reading manu-
scripts in progress by Thomas Lifka on the concept of totalitarianism and by Martin Weil on the State Department and
the origins of the Cold War.

1. *New York Times,* June 24, 1941, quoted in Gar Alperovitz, *Atomic
   Diplomacy: Hiroshima and Potsdam* (New York: Simon and Schuster, 1965), p. 30.
2. Walter Millis, ed., *The Forrestal Diaries* (New York: Viking Press,
   1951), p. 57.
3. 77 Cong., 1 sess., *Congressional Record* (Oct. 23, 1941), p. 8204.
4. Harry S. Truman, *Memoirs,* 2 vols. (Garden City, N.Y.: Doubleday, 1955–1956), I, p. 82.
5. *U.S. News and World Report,* XIX (Sept. 14, 1945), p. 76; *New
   Republic,* CXIII (August 27, 1945), p. 254.
6. Roosevelt is quoted in William C. Bullitt, "How We Won the War
   and Lost the Peace," *Life,* XXV (August 30, 1948), p. 94. In view
   of the former intimacy between Bullitt and many of the senior
   Europeanists in State, it seems highly probable that he had re-
   tailed this quotation to them long before he published it. Morgenthau's observation appears in John M. Blum, *From the Morgenthau
   Diaries,* 3 vols. (Boston: Houghton Mifflin, 1959–67), III, p. 368.
7. Joseph C. Grew, *Turbulent Era: A Diplomatic Record of Forty
   Years, 1904–1945,* 2 vols. (Boston: Houghton Mifflin, 1952), I,
   pp. 420, 506; Waldo H. Heinrichs, Jr., *American Ambassador:
   Joseph C. Grew and the Development of the American Diplomatic
   Tradition* (Boston: Little, Brown, 1966), pp. 45, 49, 186, 271,
   302–3.
8. Grew, *Turbulent Era,* II, p. 1446.
9. Ernest O. Hauser, "Something New in Striped Pants," *Saturday
   Evening Post,* CCXXII (Nov. 12, 1949), pp. 47ff.; *Nation,*
   CLXIII (Aug. 4, 1946), p. 115; *U.S. News and World Report,*
   XXXII (Feb. 8, 1952), p. 40; Dean G. Acheson, *Present at the*

Creation: My Years in the State Department (New York: W. W. Norton, 1969), p. 90; Robert Bendiner, *The Riddle of the State Department* (New York: Farrar and Rinehart, 1942), pp. 59, 184–85; Claude G. Bowers, *My Mission to Spain: Watching the Rehearsal for World War II* (New York: Simon and Schuster, 1954), p. 414; F. Jay Taylor, *The United States and the Spanish Civil War* (New York: Bookman Associates, 1956), p. 185; Joseph P. Lash, *Eleanor and Franklin* (New York: W. W. Norton, 1971), pp. 713–14; U.S. Department of State, *Foreign Relations of the United States* [hereafter *FRUS*], *1941*, I, pp. 766–67.

10. Beatrice Farnsworth, *William C. Bullitt and the Soviet Union* (Bloomington: Indiana University Press, 1967), p. 288; *PM* (July 14, 1943), p. 19; George F. Kennan, *Memoirs, 1925–1950* (Boston: Little, Brown, 1967), p. 288; *FRUS, 1946*, I, p. 1167.

11. *FRUS, The Soviet Union, 1933–1939*, pp. 514–18, 773–75; Robert E. Sherwood, *Roosevelt and Hopkins* (New York: Harper and Brothers, 1948), p. 395; *PM* (March 21, 1943), p. 5; Spruille Braden, *Diplomats and Demagogues* (New Rochelle, N.Y.: Arlington House, 1971), pp. 347–48; editorial, *Saturday Evening Post*, CCXXV (June 6, 1953), p. 10; *Fortune*, LV (March 1957), pp. 110–13.

12. See Arthur Bliss Lane, *I Saw Poland Betrayed* (Indianapolis: Bobbs-Merrill Company, 1948).

13. *FRUS, 1945*, IV, pp. 885, 901.

14. *Ibid.*, VIII, p. 1262; *ibid.*, IV, p. 352.

15. *FRUS, 1946*, I, p. 1168.

16. *Encyclopedia Britannica* (1969 edition), IV, pp. 390–92; Robert L. Wolff, *The Balkans in Our Time* (Cambridge: Harvard University Press, 1956), pp. 134–35.

17. *FRUS, 1945*, IV, pp. 191–92.

18. *Ibid.*, pp. 167, 212–14, 403 (*italics* added).

19. *Ibid.*, pp. 605, 629.

20. Harry S. Truman, *Memoirs*, 2 vols. (New York: Doubleday, 1955–56), II, p. 56.

21. Acheson, *Present at the Creation*, pp. 157–58; Harry Howe Ransom, *The Intelligence Establishment* (Cambridge: Harvard University Press, 1970), pp. 75–81.

22. *FRUS, 1946*, I, p. 1166.

23. John Lewis Gaddis, *The United States and the Origins of the Cold War, 1941–1947* (New York: Columbia University Press, 1972), pp. 230–31; Millis, *Forrestal Diaries*, p. 62.

24. Gaddis, *The United States and the Origins of the Cold War,* p. 285.

25. *FRUS, 1945,* IV, pp. 280, 422, 553, 1260, 1292.

26. Millis, *Forrestal Diaries,* pp. 95–96.

27. Richard G. Hewlett and Oscar E. Anderson, *A History of the U.S. Atomic Energy Commission,* Vol. I: *The New World, 1939–1946* (University Park, Pa.: Pennsylvania State University Press, 1962), p. 548.

28. Bernard M. Baruch, *The Public Years* (New York: Holt, Rinehart and Winston, 1960), p. 367.

29. U.S. Department of State, *State Department Bulletin,* XVI (January 19, 1947), p. 89. On the question of whether the Baruch amendments influenced the outcome, the best study is Robert Gard, "Arms Control Policy Formulation and Negotiations, 1945–1946" (Ph.D. thesis, Harvard University, 1961).

30. *FRUS, 1945,* VIII, pp. 45–48, 386–88, 1225–28.

31. *Ibid.,* pp. 15–18.

32. Kennan, *Memoirs,* p. 287.

33. *FRUS, 1945,* VIII, pp. 251–52, 508, 1248–49, 1260–62.

34. *FRUS, 1946,* VII, pp. 1–6.

35. Truman, *Memoirs,* I, p. 552.

36. *FRUS, 1946,* VII, pp. 416, 536 ff., 566.

37. *FRUS, 1946,* VII, pp. 829, 836–38.

38. Robert Greenhalgh Albion and Robert Howe Connery, *Forrestal and the Navy* (New York: Columbia University Press, 1962), pp. 186–87; Vincent Davis, *Postwar Defense Policy and the U.S. Navy, 1943–1946* (Chapel Hill: University of North Carolina Press, 1966), pp. 224–25.

39. *FRUS, 1946,* VII, pp. 857–58.

40. *Ibid.,* pp. 840–42.

41. *Ibid.,* p. 840; Acheson, *Present at the Creation,* pp. 195–96.

42. *FRUS, 1946,* VII, pp. 209–13.

43. *Ibid.,* pp. 523–25.

44. The Clifford memorandum is reproduced in Arthur Krock, *Memoirs: Sixty Years on the Firing Line* (New York: Funk and Wagnalls, 1968), pp. 419–82.

45. *FRUS, 1946,* VII, pp. 893–97.

46. Acheson, *Present at the Creation,* p. 219; Joseph Marion Jones, *The Fifteen Weeks: An Inside Account of the Genesis of the Marshall Plan* (New York: Viking Press, 1955), pp. 139–42.

47. *Public Papers of the Presidents: Harry S Truman, 1947,* pp. 176–80; 80 Cong., 1 sess., U.S. Senate, Committee on Foreign Relations, *Hearings on Assistance to Greece and Turkey,* p. 24.

48. *FRUS, 1945*, VIII, pp. 266–67.

49. Millis, *Forrestal Diaries*, p. 212; *FRUS, 1946*, VII, pp. 362–64; Kennan, *Memoirs*, pp. 313–21.

50. Gaddis, *The United States and the Origins of the Cold War*, pp. 139–49.

51. *Ibid.*, pp. 290–96, 315.

52. *Ibid.*, pp. 306–7, 312.

53. Gaddis Smith, *Dean Acheson* (New York: Cooper Square Publishers, 1972), p. 424.

54. Millis, *Forrestal Diaries*, p. 128.

III   Korea, 1950: History Overpowering Calculation

The argument of this chapter was first set forth as a hypothesis in "The Nature of Foreign Policy: The Calculated versus the Axiomatic," *Daedalus* (Fall 1962), pp. 653–67. I am grateful to Stephen R. Graubard and to Richard N. Berkman for comments on that article. In addition to those cited in the notes, other works useful for this chapter were Ronald J. Caridi, *The Korean War and American Politics: The Republican Party as a Case Study* (Philadelphia: University of Pennsylvania Press, 1968) and David Rees, *Korea: The Limited War* (London: Macmillan, 1964).

1. Memo by the Assistant to the President's Naval Aide, n.d., summarizing the contents of White House files, U.S. Department of State, *Foreign Relations of the United States* [hereafter *FRUS*], *1945: The Conference of Berlin (Potsdam)*, I, pp. 309–10.

2. *Ibid.*, II, pp. 351–52.

3. *FRUS, 1945*, VI, pp. 1037–39; J. Lawton Collins, *War in Peacetime: The History and Lessons of Korea* (Boston: Houghton Mifflin, 1969), pp. 25–26, footnote; Gregory Henderson, *Korea: The Politics of the Vortex* (Cambridge: Harvard University Press, 1968), pp. 121–22.

4. Except where otherwise noted, this paragraph and those following draw on Henderson, *Korea*, pp. 116–47.

5. *FRUS, 1945*, VI, pp. 1144–88; Harry S Truman, *Memoirs*, 2 vols. (Garden City, N.Y.: Doubleday, 1955–56), II, pp. 317–18.

6. *Current Biography, 1947*, pp. 305–8; Dean G. Acheson, *Present at the Creation: My Years in the State Department* (New York:

W. W. Norton, 1969), p. 144; 80 Cong., 1 sess., U.S. Senate, Committee on Appropriations, *Hearings on First Deficiency Appropriation Bill for 1947*, pp. 128–32.

7. *FRUS, 1945*, VI, pp. 113–14, 1127–28; *FRUS, 1946*, VIII, pp. 645–46; George M. McCune, "The Occupation of Korea," *Foreign Policy Reports*, XXIII (Oct. 15, 1947), pp. 186–95.

8. *FRUS, 1945*, VI, pp. 1137–38, 1150–51; *FRUS, 1946*, VIII, pp. 623–27, 653–56; James F. Byrnes, *Speaking Frankly* (New York: Harper and Brothers, 1947), pp. 221–23.

9. *FRUS, 1946*, VIII, pp. 619–21, 661, 681–82.

10. *Ibid.*, pp. 706–9, 713–14; Truman, *Memoirs*, II, pp. 321–22.

11. *FRUS, 1946*, VIII, pp. 721–22.

12. Letter from John Carter Vincent, *New York Times*, Jan. 30, 1957.

13. *FRUS, 1947*, VI, p. 626.

14. *Ibid.*, pp. 817–18.

15. *Ibid.*, pp. 711, 803–7, 874.

16. Robert K. Sawyer, *Military Advisors in Korea: KMAG in Peace and War* (Washington, D.C.: Office of the Chief of Military History, U.S. Army, 1962), p. 30; Collins, *War in Peacetime*, p. 29.

17. 80 Cong., 2 sess., U.S. Senate, Committee on Appropriations, *Hearings . . . on Economic Cooperation Administration*, p. 487; Sawyer, *Military Advisors in Korea*, p. 36.

18. Truman, *Memoirs*, II, p. 328.

19. Collins, *War in Peacetime*, p. 28; Truman, *Memoirs*, II, p. 329.

20. *Ibid.*, pp. 328–29; Sawyer, *Military Advisors in Korea*, pp. 38, 43.

21. *New York Times*, May 7–8, 1949; Collins, *War in Peacetime*, p. 29; Sawyer, *Military Advisors in Korea*, p. 105, footnote.

22. Collins, *War in Peacetime*, p. 30.

23. Acheson, *Present at the Creation*, pp. 303, 431–32.

24. *New York Times*, April 5, 1950; *ibid.*, Jan. 14, 1950.

25. For example, *New York Times*, June 11, 1949, and "Korea Heads for the Shoals," *Business Week* (Sept. 17, 1949), pp. 116–17.

26. 82 Cong., 2 sess., U.S. Senate, Committees on Armed Services and Foreign Relations, *The Military Situation in the Far East* [hereafter *MacArthur Hearings*], part 3, p. 1991.

27. 81 Cong., 2 sess., U.S. Senate, Committee on Appropriations, *Hearings on Foreign Aid Appropriations for 1951*, pp. 305–6.

28. Sawyer, *Military Advisors in Korea*, pp. 30, 100–101.

29. Dean G. Acheson, "Crisis in Asia—An Examination of U.S. Policy," *State Department Bulletin*, XXII (Jan. 23, 1950), pp. 111–18; Glenn D. Paige, *The Korean Decision* (New York: Free Press,

1968), p. 69, footnote, reports a 1955 interview with Rusk, discounting the strength of concern about Rhee's possible aggressiveness.

30. *MacArthur Hearings*, part 3, p. 2371.

31. *New York Times*, Jan. 22, 1950; 81 Cong., 2 sess., U.S. Senate, Committee on Appropriations, *Hearings . . . on Foreign Aid Appropriations for 1951*, pp. 334, 339; Truman, *Memoirs*, II, p. 329; Acheson, *Present at the Creation*, p. 358.

32. Paige, *Korean Decision*, p. 68.

33. Except as otherwise noted, the account of events of June 24–30 is taken from the admirable hour-by-hour chronicle in Paige, *Korean Decision*, pp. 79–272.

34. *New York Times*, June 28, 1950; Paige, *Korean Decision*, pp. 248–50.

35. Truman, *Memoirs*, II, p. 332; Acheson, *Present at the Creation*, p. 404.

36. Paige, *Korean Decision*, pp. 114, 124.

37. *Ibid.*, pp. 125–43.

38. *Ibid.*, pp. 148–49, 158, 180.

39. Joseph de Rivera, *The Psychological Dimension of Foreign Policy* (Columbus, Ohio: Charles E. Merrill, 1968), p. 125, cites this as an example of a psychological process often observable in other situations.

40. Paige, *Korean Decision*, p. 132; George F. Kennan, *Memoirs, 1925–1950* (Boston: Little, Brown, 1967), pp. 485–87. On Webb's reservations, see Paige, *op. cit.*, p. 141.

41. Sawyer, *Military Advisors in Korea*, pp. 57, 111; *MacArthur Hearings*, part 2, p. 1019.

42. *Ibid.*, pp. 159–60; James Reston, one of the best-informed and most perceptive newspapermen in Washington, assumed and reported that the United States would adopt the posture of a third party and avoid becoming an active participant: *New York Times*, June 27, 1950.

43. Paige, *Korean Decision*, pp. 45–47.

44. Richard E. Neustadt, *Presidential Power* (New York: John Wiley and Sons, 1960), p. 175. See also Cabell Phillips, *The Truman Presidency: The History of a Triumphant Succession* (New York: Macmillan, 1966), pp. 10–29.

45. Administration spokesmen had recently publicly denounced the Rhee regime as undemocratic. Although they were to speak later of defending freedom in South Korea, it seems unlikely that con-

cern for the country's institutions or the existing liberties of its
citizens constituted a major motive in the June decision. See *New
York Times*, Jan. 14, 1950; *State Department Bulletin*, XXII (April
17, 1950), p. 602; *ibid.* (April 24, 1966), pp. 10–29.

46. Truman, *Memoirs*, II, p. 339.
47. Paige, *Korean Decision*, p. 159.
48. Truman, *Memoirs*, II, p. 340.
49. Paige, *Korean Decision*, p. 141; Theodore C. Sorenson, *Decision-
    Making in the White House* (New York: Columbia University
    Press, 1963), pp. 43–44.
50. Paige, *Korean Decision*, pp. 45–47.
51. *Ibid.*, p. 45.
52. Acheson, *Present at the Creation*, p. 411.
53. Truman, *Memoirs*, II, p. 1; Neustadt, *Presidential Power*, pp. 172–
    73.
54. Paige, *Korean Decision*, p. 158; Truman, *Memoirs*, II, p. 328.
55. *Ibid.*, I, pp. 153, 189–90.
56. Bernard M. Baruch, *The Public Years* (New York: Holt, Rinehart
    and Winston, 1960), p. 368.
57. Truman, *Memoirs*, II, pp. 332–33.
58. *Ibid.*, p. 1; Paige, *Korean Decision*, p. 114.
59. *Ibid.*, pp. 178, 331.
60. *Ibid.*, pp. 151–53, 199, 220.
61. Adam B. Ulam, *Expansion and Coexistence: The History of Soviet
    Foreign Policy, 1917–67* (New York: Frederick A. Praeger, 1968),
    p. 519.
62. 78 Cong., 1 sess., *Congressional Record* (Nov. 2, 1943), p. 8993.
63. Thomas E. Lifka, "The Concept Totalitarianism for the Making of
    American Foreign Policy with Respect to the Soviet Union, 1933–
    1953," Ph.D. thesis in progress, Harvard University.

IV   Vietnam: The Bed of Procrustes

In addition to works cited in these notes, the following were
of special value to me in thinking about the subject matter of
this chapter: Chester Cooper, *The Lost Crusade: America in
Vietnam* (New York: Dodd, Mead, 1970); Daniel Ellsberg,
"Escalating in a Quagmire," *Public Policy* (Spring 1971), pp.
217–74; Leslie Gelb, "Vietnam: The System Worked," *Foreign
Policy*, II (Summer 1971), pp. 140–67, and "The Essential

Domino: American Politics and Vietnam," *Foreign Affairs*, L (April 1972), pp. 459–75; Arthur M. Schlesinger, Jr., *The Bitter Heritage: Vietnam and American Democracy 1941–1965* (Boston: Houghton Mifflin, 1967); and James C. Thomson, Jr., "How Could Vietnam Happen?" in Robert Manning and Michael Janeway, eds., *Who We Are: An ATLANTIC Chronicle of the United States and Vietnam* (Boston: Little, Brown, 1969), pp. 196–212. I am also indebted to William P. Bundy for allowing me to read an as yet untitled manuscript dealing with the United States and Asia during the 1960's and to Alexander B. Woodside for sharing with me his expertness on Vietnam.

1. Herman Finer, *Dulles over Suez* (Chicago: Quadrangle Books, 1964), is a huge potpourri of interview material. Richard E. Neustadt, *Alliance Politics* (New York: Columbia University Press, 1970) is a brief study, obviously based on much more insightful interviewing.

2. Arthur M. Schlesinger, Jr., *A Thousand Days: John F. Kennedy in the White House* (Boston: Houghton Mifflin, 1965); Theodore C. Sorenson, *Kennedy* (New York: Harper and Row, 1965). On the Cuban missile crisis: Elie Abel, *The Missile Crisis* (New York: J. B. Lippincott, 1966) and especially Graham T. Allison, *Essence of Decision: Explaining the Cuban Missile Crisis* (Boston: Little, Brown, 1971).

3. Schlesinger, *A Thousand Days*, pp. 323–38; Roger Hilsman, *To Move a Nation: The Politics of Foreign Policy in the Administration of John F. Kennedy* (Garden City, N.Y.: Doubleday, 1967), pp. 91–134.

4. *The Pentagon Papers: The Defense Department History of United States Decisionmaking on Vietnam*, 4 vols. (The Senator Gravel edition; Boston: Beacon Press, 1971), II, pp. 93–94. [Hereafter cited as *Pentagon Papers*.]

5. *Ibid.*, pp. 108–9.

6. *Ibid.*, p. 105.

7. *Ibid.*, pp. 83–84.

8. *State Department Bulletin*, XLIX (Sept. 30, 1963), p. 499.

9. *The Public Papers of the Presidents: John F. Kennedy, 1963*, pp. 17–18. A good index of then-prevailing expert opinion is A. Doak

Barnett, *Communist China and Asia, Challenge to American Policy* (New York: Vintage Books, 1960).

10. *Pentagon Papers*, II, p. 113.
11. *Ibid.*, p. 46.
12. *Ibid.*, p. 79.
13. *Ibid.*, p. 124.
14. Schlesinger, *A Thousand Days*, p. 321.
15. Richard E. Neustadt, *Presidential Power: The Politics of Leadership* (New York: John Wiley and Sons, 1960), pp. 96–97, 210–12.
16. Hilsman, *To Move a Nation*, p. 129.
17. *Ibid.*, p. 134.
18. *Pentagon Papers*, II, p. 58.
19. *Ibid.*, p. 92.
20. Schlesinger, *A Thousand Days*, pp. 540–41.
21. Sorenson, *Kennedy*, pp. 713–14.
22. *Pentagon Papers*, II, p. 650.
23. Robert S. McNamara, "United States Policy in Viet-Nam," *State Department Bulletin*, L (April 13, 1964), pp. 562–70; *Pentagon Papers*, II, p. 305.
24. *Ibid.*, p. 111.
25. *State Department Bulletin*, XLIX (Sept. 30, 1963), p. 499.
26. *Pentagon Papers*, II, p. 664.
27. *Ibid.*, pp. 36, 74–75.
28. *Ibid.*, p. 107.
29. *Pentagon Papers*, II, pp. 263–64.
30. *Ibid.*, III, pp. 50–51.
31. *State Department Bulletin*, L (June 8, 1964), p. 890.
32. *Ibid.* (Oct. 19, 1964), p. 537.
33. *Pentagon Papers*, III, p. 696.
34. *Ibid.*, p. 625.
35. Allen S. Whiting, *China Crosses the Yalu: The Decision To Enter the Korean War* (Stanford, Calif.: Stanford University Press, 1960); information from William P. Bundy.
36. *Pentagon Papers,* III, p. 320.
37. *Ibid.*, p. 581; *ibid.*, IV, p. 220.
38. *Ibid.*, III, p. 623.
39. *Ibid.*, p. 617.
40. *Ibid.*, p. 648.
41. *Ibid.*, II, p. 322.
42. Lyndon Baines Johnson, *The Vantage Point: Perspectives on the*

Presidency, 1963–1969 (New York: Holt, Rinehart and Winston, 1971), p. 123.

43. *Pentagon Papers*, III, p. 696.
44. *Ibid.*, pp. 623, 631.
45. *State Department Bulletin*, L (June 8, 1964), p. 908.
46. *Public Papers of the Presidents: Lyndon B. Johnson, 1963–1964*, II, p. 930.
47. *Pentagon Papers*, III, pp. 582–83.
48. *Ibid.*, p. 657.
49. *Ibid.*, p. 624.
50. George W. Ball, "Top Secret: The Prophecy the President Rejected," *Atlantic Monthly*, CCXXX (July 1972), pp. 35–49.
51. *Pentagon Papers*, III, p. 683.
52. *Ibid.*, p. 647.
53. *Ibid.*, pp. 381–82.
54. *Ibid.*, p. 314.
55. Johnson, *Vantage Point*, p. 152.
56. *State Department Bulletin*, LI (June 7, 1965), p. 922.
57. Johnson, *Vantage Point*, pp. 46–47.
58. *Public Papers of the Presidents: Lyndon B. Johnson, 1965*, I, p. 449.
59. *Pentagon Papers*, III, pp. 498, 502.
60. *Ibid.*, p. 419.
61. Allison, *Essence of Decision*, pp. 10–38.
62. *Pentagon Papers*, IV, p. 173.
63. For example, Joseph Buttinger, *The Smaller Dragon: A Political History of Vietnam* (New York: Praeger, 1958).

V Analysis: Bombing for Peace

A version of this material was composed in 1966 and circulated privately. Many friends were kind enough to comment on it, among them Graham T. Allison, Martin Blumenson, Robert J. C. Butow, Ramsey Clark, Franklin L. Ford, Ernest H. Giusti, William R. Harris, H. Stuart Hughes, Fred C. Iklé, William W. Kaufmann, Henry A. Kissinger, Colonel George A. Lincoln, John M. H. Lindbeck, Robert A. Lovett, Andrew W. Marshall, Maurice Matloff, John D. Montgomery, Jonathan Moore, Richard E. Neustadt, Ithiel de Sola Pool, George Quester, Admiral Arthur W. Radford, Thomas C. Schelling, Marshall D. Shulman, James C. Thomson, Jr., Samuel R. Williamson, Jr., and Adam Yarmolinsky. I am grateful to all of them.

Some works not cited in the notes upon which this chapter draws are Bernard Brodie, *Strategic Air Power in World War II* (Santa Monica, Calif.: RAND Corporation, 1957); Fred C. Iklé, *The Social Impact of Bomb Destruction* (Norman: University of Oklahoma Press, 1958); Irving L. Janis, *Air War and Emotional Stress* (Santa Monica, Calif.: RAND Corporation, 1951); George Quester, *Deterrence before Hiroshima* (New York: John Wiley and Sons, 1966); and Thomas C. Schelling, *Arms and Influence* (New Haven: Yale University Press, 1966).

1. *The Pentagon Papers: The Defense Department History of United States Decisionmaking on Vietnam,* 4 vols. (The Senator Gravel edition; Boston: Beacon Press, 1971), III, p. 313. [Hereafter referred to as *Pentagon Papers.*]

2. *Ibid.,* p. 289.

3. 90 Cong., 1 sess., House of Representatives, Committee on Armed Services, *Fiscal Year 1967 Supplementary Authorization for Southeast Asia,* p. 145.

4. *Pentagon Papers,* III, pp. 214–15.

5. Interrogation No. 428 (Nov. 23, 1945), U.S. Strategic Bombing Survey, *Japanese Air Power* (Washington, D.C.: U.S. Strategic Bombing Survey, 1946).

6. Maurice Matloff, *Strategic Planning for Coalition Warfare, 1943–1944* (Washington, D.C.: Office of the Chief of Military History, Department of the Army, 1959), p. 28.

7. In describing these three instances, I rely, except where otherwise noted, on the following. For Italy: Gianfranco Bianchi, *25 iuglio, crollo di un regima* (Milan: U. Murcia, 1963); F. W. Deakin, *The Brutal Friendship: Mussolini, Hitler and the Fall of Italian Fascism* (New York: Harper and Row, 1962); Albert N. Garland and Howard McGaw Smyth, *Sicily and the Surrender of Italy* (Washington, D.C.: Office of the Chief of Military History, Department of the Army, 1965); Ruggero Zangrando, *1943: 25 iuglio–8 settembre* (Milan: Feltrinelli, 1964); For Japan: Lester Brooks, *Behind Japan's Surrender: The Secret Struggle That Ended an Empire* (New York: McGraw-Hill, 1968); Robert J. C. Butow,

Japan's Decision to Surrender (Stanford: Stanford University Press, 1954); Wesley Frank Craven and James Lea Cate, eds., *The Army Air Forces in World War II* 5 vols. (Chicago: University of Chicago Press, 1949–53), IV and V; Japan, Ministry of Foreign Affairs, *Shūsen Shiroku* [History of the Termination of the War] (Tokyo, 1952), of which Dr. Fred C. Iklé supplied me an English translation; and United States Strategic Bombing Survey, *Japan's Struggle To End the War* (Washington, D.C.: Government Printing Office, 1946). For the Korean War: Robert Frank Futtrell, *The United States Air Force in Korea, 1950–1953* (New York: Duell, Sloan and Pearce, 1961); Walter G. Hermes, *Truce Tent and Fighting Front* (Washington, D.C.: Office of the Chief of Military History, Department of the Army, 1966); Robert A. Scalapino, ed., *North Korea Today* (New York: Praeger, 1963); and James T. Stewart, ed., *Airpower: The Decisive Force in Korea* (Princeton: Van Nostrand, 1957).

8. Paolo Puntoni, *Parla Vittorio Emmanuele III* (Milan: Aldo Palazzi, 1958), p. 140.

9. Butow, *Japan's Decision To Surrender*, p. 67.

10. Benito Mussolini, *The Fall of Mussolini* (English translation; New York: Farrar, Straus, 1948), p. 61.

11. Butow, *Japan's Decision To Surrender*, p. 47.

12. Hugh Gibson, ed., *The Ciano Diaries* (Garden City, N.Y.: Doubleday, 1946), pp. 510–14, 521–28, 533, 537–38, 545.

13. Ivanoe Bonomi, *Diario di un anno (2 giugno 1943–10 giugno 1944)* (Cernusco sul Naviglio: Garzanti, 1947), pp. xxi–xxxviii.

14. Toshikazu Kase, *Journey to the Missouri*, ed. by David Nelson Rowe (New Haven: Yale University Press, 1950), pp. 75–76, 81.

15. Kase, *Journey to the Missouri*, p. 78.

16. Peter S. H. Tang, *Communist China Today* (New York: Praeger, 1957), pp. 81–94.

17. Leonard Schapiro, *The Communist Party of the Soviet Union* (New York: Random House, 1960), pp. 542–46.

18. Patrick J. Honey, *North Vietnam Today: Profile of a Communist Satellite* (New York: Praeger, 1962).

VI Prediction: U.S. Foreign Policy in the Next Decade

An early version of this chapter was presented orally before a student audience at North Carolina State College. I am grateful to Professor John Gilbert of that institution for his invitation and prompting and to various members of the audience for their questions. In addition, I am indebted to Leslie Gelb of the Brookings Institution for helpful comments on the manuscript.

1. I have attempted to summarize the enormous literature on "the foreign policy public" in "An American Tradition in Foreign Policy: The Role of Public Opinion," in William H. Nelson, ed., *Theory and Practice in American Politics* (Chicago: University of Chicago Press, 1964), pp. 101–22.

2. V. O. Key, *Public Opinion and American Democracy* (New York: Knopf, 1961), pp. 173–74.

3. Kenneth P. Adler and Davis Bobrow, "Interest and Influence in Foreign Affairs," *Public Opinion Quarterly*, XX (Spring 1956), pp. 89–101.

4. Richard Rovere, "Notes on the Establishment in America," *American Scholar*, XXX (Autumn 1961), pp. 489–95.

5. James N. Rosenau, *National Leadership and Foreign Policy: A Case Study in the Mobilization of Public Support* (Princeton: Princeton University Press, 1963), pp. 30–31, 331–62.

6. Elie Abel, *The Missile Crisis* (New York: Lippincott, 1966), p. 38.

7. Adam Yarmolinsky, *The Military Establishment: Its Impacts on American Society* (New York: Harper and Row, 1971), pp. 131–32.

8. The process is detailed in a forthcoming study by John D. Steinbruner.

9. "The Limits of Commitment: A *Time*-Louis Harris Poll," *Time*, XCIII (May 2, 1969), pp. 16–17; "Not So Hawkish: The Results of Polls on Military Spending," *Nation*, CCXI (Oct. 19, 1970), p. 354.

VII   Tasks for Historians

Some points in this chapter coincide with points in my article, "A Case for 'Court Historians,'" *Perspectives in American History*, III (1969), pp. 413–34. Both this chapter and that article owe a special debt to Richard L. Berkman, who in the summer of 1967 interviewed on my behalf a number of government officials. It also owes debts not acknowledged in notes below to Arthur M. Schlesinger, Jr., "The Historian and History,"

Foreign Affairs, XLI (April 1963), pp. 491–97; Herbert Feis, "The Shackled Historian," *ibid.,* XLV (Jan. 1967), pp. 332–43; and Francis L. Loewenheim, ed., *The Historian and the Diplomat: The Role of History and Historians in American Foreign Policy* (New York: Harper and Row, 1967).

1. See, for example, *The Pentagon Papers: The Defense Department History of United States Decisionmaking in Vietnam,* 4 vols. (The Senator Gravel edition; Boston: Beacon Press, 1971), II, p. 69; III, pp. 101, 206, 303; IV, pp. 77, 89–90, 414–15.

2. *Ibid.,* III, p. 500.

3. *Ibid.,* IV, pp. 89–90.

4. Walter Millis, ed., *The Forrestal Diaries* (New York: Viking Press, 1951), p. 62; Arthur M. Schlesinger, Jr., *A Thousand Days: John F. Kennedy in the White House* (Boston: Houghton Mifflin, 1965), p. 406.

5. Zara S. Steiner, *The Foreign Office and Foreign Policy, 1898–1914* (Cambridge: Cambridge University Press, 1969), p. 22.

6. Richard Koebner and Helmut Dan Schmidt, *Imperialism: The Story and Significance of a Political Word, 1840–1960* (Cambridge: Cambridge University Press, 1964).

7. Arthur M. Schlesinger, Jr., *The Bitter Heritage: Vietnam and American Democracy* (Boston: Houghton Mifflin, 1966), p. 91.

8. Executive Order 11652, March 8, 1972, reproduced in Carol M. Barker and Matthew T. Fox, *Classified Files: The Yellowing Pages* (New York: Twentieth Century Fund, 1972), pp. 97–105.

9. *Ibid.,* pp. 89–90.

10. William L. Langer and S. Everett Gleason, *The Challenge to Isolation, 1937–1940* (New York: Harper and Brothers, 1952) and *The Undeclared War, 1940–1941* (New York: Harper and Brothers, 1953); Herbert Feis, *The China Tangle: The American Effort in China from Pearl Harbor to the Marshall Mission* (Princeton: Princeton University Press, 1953).

11. Barker and Fox, *Classified Files,* p. 72.

12. Berkman interview.

Index

DATE DUE